Society, Language, and
the University

Society, Language, and the University

From Lenny Bruce to Noam Chomsky

Sol Saporta

VANTAGE PRESS
New York

FIRST EDITION

Copyright © 1994 by Sol Saporta

Published by Vantage Press, Inc.
516 West 34th Street, New York, New York 10001

Manufactured in the United States of America
ISBN: 0-533-10702-4

Library of Congress Catalog Card No.: 93-93968

0 9 8 7 6 5 4 3 2

Remembering Joe, Raquel, and Wendy

Contents

Introduction

The subtitle of this collection, "From Lenny Bruce to Noam Chomsky," is not intended to be frivolous. I would be surprised if either had ever seen the other, and yet they share certain insights and integrity that I think would have impressed the other. Bruce was funny, but he was also smart. Chomsky is smart, but he can also be funny.

Regardless, they are good representatives of my own interests over the years. My career as a stand-up comic lasted one evening. When I was a freshman at C.C.N.Y. in 1940, a group of us put on a show, which I think was called, "Mirth, Magic, and Music." I was Mirth. On the other hand, I taught linguistics for thirty-five years: five years at Indiana University and thirty years at the University of Washington. As far as time is concerned, the asymmetry does not adequately reflect the significance I attach to the two types of enterprise. Getting someone to laugh (for the right reason) seems to me just as worthwhile as most forms of scholarly inquiry. I wish I had had more talent at the first.

My feelings about academia are typified by a conversation I had with a student some years ago. By chance, we had both recently read *Cat's Cradle,* by Kurt Vonnegut, Jr. In it, Vonnegut distinguishes between two types of groups. The first consists of people who have genuine emotional ties to one another, who experience one another's joy and suffering, a type of family that Vonnegut called "a kurass." The other group shares only superficial features in common, groups that Vonnegut called "a granfaloon." Members of the Elks Club, and people from Texas, he said, constitute a granfaloon. In the course of our discussion about the university, the student said, "The trouble with you,

Sol, is that you want the Department of Linguistics to be a kurass, but it's really a granfaloon." I think he was right on both scores.

Society, Language, and
the University

PART I

CONTEMPORARY CULTURE

1

Jackie Robinson: Our Heroes, As We See Them*

My recollection of the year 1948 is that the two activities that occupied most of my time and energy were rooting for Jackie Robinson and the Brooklyn Dodgers, and campaigning for Henry Wallace, the Progressive Party candidate for president who was challenging both Harry Truman and Thomas E. Dewey.

Some time between then and now I came to understand that, in its own way, the first of these commitments was just as political as the second.

The impact of the integration of professional athletics hardly needs additional documentation. But it is hard to over-estimate the effect it had on young New York sports fans who perceived themselves as some kind of leftists.

The debate between Dodger fans and Yankee fans now took on a moral dimension that it had never had before. Rooting for the National League in the All-Star game was a commitment to racial justice in the form of a roster that included blacks and Latinos. Our sense of self-righteousness, naive and misguided as it may have been, was nevertheless based on facts that were indisputable.

So far, so good. But, now things start getting fuzzy. The

*Originally published under the title "Our Heroes, As We See Them." *Against the Current* (May/June 1988): p. 2. Reprinted with permission.

reality generates its own fantasy. Simply put, my illusion, one that I have never been able to relinquish completely (Where have you gone, Joe DiMaggio?) is that I wanted my heroes to be better than they were.

I was pretty good at resisting most of the illusions, both romantic and non-romantic, that are promoted in this society. I don't remember ever really believing in Santa Claus (or God); I didn't believe my mother when she told me she got me at Macy's; and reading in a history book that George Washington never told a lie didn't strengthen my faith in George Washington or the American presidency. It just made me suspicious of the trust-worthiness of history books.

And the romantic quest for that blissful relationship between two persons, each caring, considerate, committed, compassionate, living out their lives in passionate heterosexual monogamy, evolving harmoniously into the indefinite future—that quest never captured my imagination. Never? Well—hardly ever.

But—I did seek something from the athletes and performers that I revered. It was not enough for them to have artistic talent or athletic skills.

I wanted them to have intelligence, integrity and, most important, a social conscience. And, even more, I wanted those qualities to be so completely integrated into their lives and beings that a knowledgeable fan could occasionally discern the expression of those qualities in their artistic or athletic performance.

Robinson could bunt, steal bases, hit for average, bat in runs and make the double play. How could he fail to understand the predatory nature of monopoly capitalism?

So it was not merely an irony and a disappointment when a few years later Robinson publicly supported Nelson Rockefeller; it was close to betrayal. If there was one name that one could identify as epitomizing the institutions that prevented this society from approximating any genuine egalitarianism, that name was probably Rockefeller.

And, similarly, for the entertainers. *Casablanca* was prob-

4

ably my all-time favorite movie from the time it appeared until *Annie Hall* replaced it at the top of my list. I was too old to be devastated or even terribly surprised, but I have never been able to reconcile my emotional response to the film with the fact that Humphrey Bogart apparently had spent much of one of his early marriages beating up his wife.

The erroneous basis of my illusion seems clear. In my world, there would be some systematic correlation between beauty and grace on the one hand, and virtue on the other. It would reassure the child in all of us if truth, beauty and virtue somehow converged. In this world they are independent, and when they co-occur, it's coincidence.

It is now a cliché to observe that entertainers and athletes are the royalty of our society. Somehow, I have failed to draw the obvious conclusion: our royalty can't also be our revolutionaries.

2

Lenny Bruce's Views on Language*

Lenny Bruce was quite explicit about his views on linguistic taboos. There were two main arguments to his position: first, that taboo words constituted a form of word magic, and a society that tolerated word magic was pathological; and second, that the obvious way to eliminate taboos, perhaps the only way, was by repeated usage.

There are two routines which are particularly relevant in assessing his understanding of taboo words and how they function. One is *To is a preposition; come is a verb;* the other is *Blah blah blah.*

Consider the following text (excerpted from the printed version; Cohen 1967: 189–190):[1]

"*Tooooooooo*
    is a preposition
To is a preposition
Commmmmme
    is a verb.
To is a preposition,
Come is a verb.
To is a preposition,
Come is a verb, the verb intransitive.
To

*Originally published in *Humor* 4 (1991): pp. 133–38. Reprinted with permission of Mouton De Gruyter, a division of Walter de Gruyter & Co.

Come.
To Come. . . .

"To come to come, come too come too, to come to come uh uh uh
uh uh um um um um um uh uh uh uh uh—TO COME! TO COME!
TO COME! TO COME!
     Did you come?
     Did you come good?
     Did you come good?
     Did you come?
     Good.
To
Come.
To
Come—

     Didyoucomegood?didyoucomegoooddidyoucomegood? . . .

"Don't come in me,
don't comeinme,
don't comeinme mimme.
Don't comeinme mimme memme.
Don't comeinme mimme mimme.
Mimme.
     Comeinme.
     Comeinme.
     Comeinmecomeinmecomeinme—
     *COME*inme!
Don't comeinme mimme,
don't comeinme—

"If anyone in this room finds that verb intransitive, to come,
obscene, vile, vulgar—if it's really a hang-up to hear it and you
think I'm the rankest for saying it—*you* probably can't come. . . .

"I bet a lot of censors can't come."

     I do not wish to exaggerate Bruce's linguistic sophistication,
but it is hard not to note his awareness of the syntactic and

7

phonological features of the lexical item *come*, as well as its meaning and usage. Providing the grammatical information about word class (preposition, verb intransitive) is merely to underline what for Bruce is critical: these, after all, are merely words. What could be more innocuous and unemotional than a word's syntactic features?

In addition, words have sound. But sound is, in itself, meaningless (mimme) or subject to various permutations, with corresponding differences in meaning (to come, come too).

In short, the linguistic exercise reflects Bruce's understanding that the emotional charge associated with taboo words is completely independent of their syntactic and phonological status. In fact, he could have added that connotation is not solely a function of what the word refers to, either. *To come* is a taboo word in a way that the more or less synonymous *to have an orgasm* is not.

The second text is also illuminating (185–87):

> "I was arrested for obscenity in San Francisco for using a ten-letter word which is sort of chic. I'm not going to repeat the word tonight. It starts with a 'c.'
>
> "They said it was vernacular for a favorite homosexual practice—which is weird, cause I don't relate that word to homosexuals. It relates to any contemporary woman I know or would know or would love or would marry. But they got hung up with faggotry. All right. . . .
>
> "Now, get into court, take fingerprints. The judge? A tough outside *verbissener.*[2] Tough-o. Right? He comes in:
> "Blah-blah-blah. Siddown.
> "Swear the heat in.
> " 'What did he say?'
> " 'Your Honor, he said blah-blah-blah.'
> "The judge:
> " 'He said *blah-blah-blah?!*'
> "Then the guy really *yentaed* it up:
> " 'That's right. I couldn't believe it. Up on the stage, in front of women and a mixed audience, he said *blah-blah-blah.*'

"The judge: " 'This, I never heard, blah-blah-blah. He said *blah-blah-blah?*'

" 'He said, *blah-blah-blah!* I'm not going to lie to ya.' It's in the minutes—'I'm not gonna lie to ya.' All right. The D.A.:

" 'The guy said blah-blah-blah. Look at him. He's *smug*. He's not gonna repent. He's *glad* he said blah-blah-blah!'

"Then I dug something: they sort of *liked* saying blah-blah-blah. Because they said it a few extra times. They really got *so* involved, saying blah-blah-blah. The bailiff is yelling, 'What'd he say?'

" '*Shut up*, you blah-blah-blah.'

"They were *yelling* it in the court.

" 'He said blah-blah-blah.'

" '*Blah-blah-blah!*'

" '*Goddamn!* It's *good* to say blah-blah-blah.'

" '*That blah-blah-blah!*' "

First, it is clear that repeated use of the code word *blah blah blah* is inoffensive, whereas one mention of the taboo word *cocksucker* constitutes the basis for arrest. Since the substitution is absolutely explicit, here, again, it cannot be the reference of the word that is at issue but the emotional charge attached to one word in particular.

Incidentally, Bruce is quite astute in his observation that the word's *use* generally assumes reference to homosexuals in spite of the fact that the *meaning* is perfectly compatible with either a reference to homosexual men or heterosexual women. In short, the word is sexist in a rather unique way.

Second, in the recorded version, Bruce adds a little gratuitous, and erroneous, grammatical information: "It's two nouns and a preposition." The function, I presume, is the same as before: nothing could be more uninteresting than a technical analysis of a word's syntactic properties.[3]

Furthermore, each of the two routines suggests Bruce's views on society's perceptions of and reactions to linguistic taboos. In the first, he is quite explicit: "If it's really a hang-up to hear it . . . *you* probably can't come." That is, if the audience is uncomfortable, then, the audience has a problem. Although, clearly, it is his intent to make the audience feel uncomfortable. Or, elsewhere (217) " . . . if that word stimulated you sexually, well, you're in a lot of trouble, Jim."

Similarly, the judge and bailiff and D.A. are all hypocritical. "They sort of *liked* saying blah-blah-blah." They exploited the opportunity to say it "a few extra times."

Now, it is obvious that certain words carry an emotional charge, quite apart from their meaning, what is sometimes referred to by linguists as a word's expressive function rather than its referential function. (The word *hate* has an emotional charge that is referential, not expressive.) What is less obvious is whether, as Bruce implies, such emotional reactions are irrational. Words are symbolic (" . . . the word itself is of no consequence" [176]), but they are not *merely* symbolic.

For Bruce, however, it is clear that the existence of linguistic taboos is a social flaw, and that they should be eliminated. And, elsewhere (193), in connection with the recent publication of *Webster's Third Unabridged Dictionary*, he provides his views on how this is to be achieved:

> "Those words are now liberated from shame. They're in the dictionary now, finally. And the reason they came to the dictionary, finally, was through continual usage. Enough guys said to their wives, 'YOU CUNT' . . .
>
> "And that's why it's in the dictionary now: c-u-n-t."
>
> Or, in connection with racial epithets:

> " . . . the word's suppression gives it the power, the violence, the viciousness. If President Kennedy got on television and said, 'Tonight I'd like to introduce the niggers in my cabinet,' " the word wouldn't "mean anything any more . . . you'd never make any four-year-old nigger cry when he came home from school" (12).

But here, I think that Bruce is less convincing. It is true that words sometimes are defused as a result of a conscious decision regarding their use; consider the recent, obvious attempt to reduce the emotional charge of the word *condom*. But

10

linguistic engineering is rarely effective. In particular, breaking a taboo, even repeatedly breaking a taboo, is not the same as eliminating a taboo, whether it's a taboo act or a taboo word.

Notes

1. John Cohen, ed., *The Essential Lenny Bruce* (New York: Bell Publishing Company, 1967).
2. Bruce's use of Yiddish raises a quite different linguistic issue. He apparently had a very limited knowledge of the language, but he insisted in using it, implying that he was more fluent than he was, presumably to focus on his Jewishness, an issue that was the focus of a number of bits, e.g., "I'm Jewish . . . Eddie Cantor's *goyish* . . . Pumpernickel is Jewish, and, as you know, white bread is very *goyish*." (31)
3. The routine about "dirty toilet jokes" is based on the syntactic ambiguity reflected in the two parsings of the expression: ([dirty toilet] jokes) "a joke about dirty toilets" and (dirty [toilet jokes]) " a dirty joke about toilets."

3

Lenny Bruce on Police Brutality*

The Rodney King verdict has generated innumerable attempts at journalistic analysis, with more to come. Much of it is reducible to a debate over whether "two wrongs make a right" and other sanctimonious pronouncements about poverty, racism, police brutality, and the failure of the system of criminal justice.

I would like to suggest that the discussion include an insight about law enforcement that was made by Lenny Bruce over twenty-five years ago. The following is from *The Essential Lenny Bruce* (edited by John Cohen, 1970, pp. 207–9):

> "I figure, when it started, they said, 'Well, we're gonna have to have some rules . . . I tell you what we'll do. We'll have a vote. We'll sleep in Area A . . . We'll eat in Area B . . . We'll throw a crap in Area C.'
>
> "One night everybody was sleeping, one guy woke up. *Pow!* He got a faceful of crap, and he said:
>
> " 'Hey, what's the deal, here, I thought we had a rule. . .
>
> " 'We'll have to do something to enforce the provisions, to give it some teeth. Here's the deal: If anybody throws any crap on us while we're sleeping, they get thrown in the craphouse. Agreed? . . .'
>
> " 'Hey, wait a minute. Though we made the rule, how're we gonna get somebody to throw somebody in the craphouse? We need somebody to enforce it—law enforcement.'

*In press. Scheduled to appear in *Humor* 7 (1994): pp. 175–77. Used with permission of Mouton de Gruyter, a division of Walter de Gruyter & Co.

"Now they put this sign up on the wall, 'WANTED, LAW ENFORCEMENT.' Guys applied for the job:

" 'Look. Here's our problem, see; we're trying to get some sleep and people keep throwing crap on us. Now we want somebody to throw them right in the craphouse. And I'm delegated to do the hiring here, and, ah, here's what the job is.

" 'You see, they won't go in the craphouse by themselves. And we all agreed on the rule, now, and we firmed it up . . . we're gonna throw them right in the craphouse.

" 'But ya see, I can't do it cause I do business with these assholes, and it looks bad for me, you know, ah . . . so I want somebody to do it for me, you know? So I tell you what: Here's a stick and a gun and *you* do it—but wait till I'm out of the room. And, whenever it happens, see, I'll wait back here and I'll watch, you know, and you make sure you kick 'em in the ass and throw 'em in there.

" 'Now you'll hear me say a lotta times that it takes a certain kind of mentality to do that work, you know, and all that bullshit, you know, but you understand, it's all horseshit and you just kick 'em in the ass and make sure it's done . . . ' "

Bruce understood what none of our politicians or journalists have come to grips with, namely, that the trouble with the notion of police brutality is that it absolves the rest of us.

And Bruce foresaw, too, something about the nature of the protest:

"So what happens? Now comes the riot, or the marches—everybody is wailing, screaming. And you got a guy there, who's standing with a short-sleeved shirt on and a stick in his hand, and the people are yelling, 'Gestapo! Gestapo!' at him:

" '*Gestapo*? You asshole, I'm the *mailman!*'

"That's another big problem. People can't separate the authority and the people who have the authority vested in them . . . actually the people are demonstrating not against Vietnam [in 1992, read *racism*]—they're demonstrating against the police department. Actually, against policemen. Because they have that concept—that the law and the law enforcement are one."

(Clearly, with the King verdict, the issue is complicated by the fact that it was the law enforcers who committed the criminal acts, so that it seemed quite appropriate to demonstrate "against policemen.")

Whatever "healing the wounds" may mean, it is more likely to be effective if it incorporates Bruce's views of the issues involved.

4

Frank Sinatra: Artistry and Ideology

It is now generally agreed that Frank Sinatra just does not sing as well as he used to. Someone more knowledgeable than I about music and voice could surely document that judgment with references to timbre, phrasing, range, and other technical indicators. And, yet, somehow, the assessment in terms of his talent seems largely besides the point. The fact is that many of us just don't like Sinatra any more.

It is instructive in this regard for me to listen to Billie Holiday's last recordings, where her voice had clearly deteriorated, and to compare my reactions to that album with my feelings about the later Sinatra recordings. Listening for example, to Holiday's *Lady in Satin* is painful, evoking a sense of loss and compassion. One grieves at the change in her voice the way one grieves at the sickness of an old friend. But listening to today's Sinatra is quite different; not only does it provide very little pleasure, but in fact I'm almost embarrassed to admit that I used to like him so much.

What is unclear is how much of this reaction is a response to his talent and how much is related to Sinatra the person. How does one draw the line?

I remember reading a few years ago that while he was playing the role of Perry Mason, Raymond Burr used to get invitations to speak about the law. Of course, it seemed absurd to me that anyone could somehow attribute qualities of the character to the player, confuse the role with the performer. And yet, my changing perception of Sinatra is somehow the result of the interaction between his performance and what I read about him in the paper, and more interestingly my belief that I can discern evidence of the latter in the former. Sinatra has become arrogant and smug, complacent and self-satisfied, and his singing now betrays him. As Gregory Sandow (1987)[1] points out in a recent review of an album of six LPs, "the problem with the later Sinatra . . . is Sinatra himself."

I agree with Sandow that Sinatra is "smug" in "It was a Very Good Year," "predatory" in "Hello Young Lovers," "angry" and "contempt[uous]" in his reference to "chicks" in "Ol' MacDonald." It is easy to agree that "Sinatra hasn't always been the nicest of guys."

But there was a time when I must have thought he was, or at least, that if he wasn't, it didn't matter. Even now, listening to the first Tommy Dorsey records, "I'll Never Smile Again" and "This Love of Mine," or "All or Nothing at All" with Harry James, it is hard to perceive anything but sincerity, a straightforwardness and authenticity that were precisely the mark of Sinatra's genius. The 1945 version of "Try a Little Tenderness," as opposed to the later version, contains no hint of cynicism but only consideration and affection, even given the paternalistic and condescending nature of the lyrics. I'm not making a statement here about Sinatra's psyche or his intentions. Isn't it true that a perfect counterfeit, by definition, is indistinguishable from the real article?

Which brings us to Sinatra and sex. When I was listening to these records forty years ago, we used to refer to it as "music to get laid by." Sandow observes that "his singing . . . felt then as if it embodied dangerous, subversive sex." I would merely add that then, for Sinatra's audience, and now, for whoever the analogous star is, the words *dangerous, subversive* are redundant, all the rhetoric of the so-called sexual revolution to the contrary notwithstanding.

But what has changed is that in the early renditions, sex and romance were inextricably entwined. Indeed, it is this early commitment to the romantic dream that helps account for the evolution into the contemporary Sinatra that we all know and hate. Cynicism and contempt are the predictable backlash of an ideal betrayed. "All or Nothing at All." What could be more explicit? (Who is more vicious than the dedicated former communist?) If the early Sinatra had completely internalized the "myth of love so ideal it brings happiness all by itself," then the later Sinatra's motto must surely be something like "Do it to them before they do it to you."

If it is the case that the change in Sinatra's singing is largely the reflection of the change in Sinatra himself, then surely we may ask similar questions about other performers. I always had the idea that I was better able to understand Bing Crosby's decision to stay unhappily married to his first wife after seeing his performance as a Catholic priest. Isn't there some connection between Vanessa Redgrave's politics and her compelling characterization of *Julia*? This is not the usual polemic about the connection between politics and art. It is not even the same as asking what we can conclude about Wagner from the fact that Hitler liked him. Rather it is like asking where Hamlet ends and where Olivier begins. There seems to be a fuzzy area where the distinction becomes blurred.

Note

1. Gregory Sandow, "Tough Love," *Village Voice*, January 13, 1987, pp. 71–73.

5

Marilyn Monroe: Sexual Exploitation or Sexual Emancipation?

Now, thirty years after her death, interest in Marilyn Monroe continues, and indeed has widened to include the academic community. One of the most recent discussions is Judith Mayne's article on feminist film theory,[1] triggered by the appearance of *Marilyn*,[2] a book by Gloria Steinem on the life and career of Marilyn Monroe. Each has her own set of assumptions and priorities, both intellectual and political.

So, Steinem's focus is obvious: Monroe's "vulnerability" is referred to no less than ten times in the first twenty-three pages. Similarly for Mayne; there are twenty references to "feminist film theory/theorists" in a five-page article. Let me make my own biases explicit: first, the systematic ambiguity of a term like *feminist* (or, analogously, *Marxist*) to refer both to a way of knowing ("feminist scholarship/analysis/theory") and to a way of acting ("feminist movement") has had quite predictable, undesirable consequences. I do not know which is cause and which is effect, but the deterioration of the women's movement is related to its assimilation into the academy. As feminist (and Marxist and ethnic) studies have become more respectable academically, they have become more innocuous politically. The admirable, subversive elements of women's studies have become virtually unrecognizable. University administrators in the sixties and seventies used to moan about the "politicization of the academy." With their characteristic hypocrisy, they were off by exactly 180 degrees. The real tragedy has been the "academicization" of political movements.[3]

Second, according to Mayne, the question that haunts Steinem's book is "Can Marilyn Monroe be saved for feminism?" The question is of some interest, and I think the answer may in fact be yes, but not by exaggerating Monroe's acting talent, nor by giving her credit for a social conscience that at best was superficial,[4] nor by emphasizing the similarities between her and other women, all of which Steinem, with her newfound solidarity, does; nor by reducing Monroe to little more than the object of the male voyeur, or to a representation of "the absence of women from the film-going experience" (15), as Mayne, the feminist film theorist, does. The sexual politics of Monroe's persona cannot be reduced merely to that of "woman as the object of the look" (15).

For Steinem, Monroe is "two parts talent, one part victim, and one part joke" (13). The trouble with this analysis is that given Steinem's sexual politics, this characterization would apply to virtually any woman in our society. Not surprisingly, then, Steinem's attempt at empathy results in her converting "the real Marilyn," to whom the book is dedicated, into Everywoman. In fact, the identification is virtually made explicit in the dedication: "To the real Marilyn. And to the reality in us all." This disturbs Mayne, the feminist critic, who sees it as "the persistence of the myth of the female screen image" (14).

Clearly, Steinem did not always feel this close to Monroe. Indeed, in 1953, she was embarrassed by the "whispering, simpering, big-breasted child-woman" (3) that she saw in *Gentlemen Prefer Blondes*.

But in 1986, Monroe's "vulnerability" has transformed her into Steinem's sister, as indicated by an explicit comparison of Monroe to Steinem when the latter was "vulnerable and unconfident" (3). Or, later on, Marilyn is said to be a typical product of this society, "hoping that a relationship with a man would give her the identity she lacked" (118).

In keeping with her attempt to be understanding and sympathetic, indeed, to make sense of all of Monroe's faults, Steinem bends over backwards not to be critical. To take just one example, Steinem seems almost to admire Monroe's use of sex to further her career: "Marilyn supplied sex so that she would be allowed to work, but not so that she wouldn't have to work" (69); she cites with apparent approval what Monroe considered a source of considerable pride: "I've never been a kept woman" (64). This is a strangely moralistic view of both work and sex on the part of someone who presumably advocates an egalitarian society premised on the emancipation of women. What does this say, for example, about prostitution, where a woman's work is sex, or about unhappy marriages, where sex is often work? This was, of course, before the 90s, when sexual harassment has become the focal point of the new feminism, and when it is common for feminists to advocate a form of sexual apartheid in the workplace. One can only speculate about what Monroe's view of that position might be.

According to Steinem, the interest in Monroe continues because of her "premature" death. She observes that we are more interested in James Dean than we are in Gary Cooper, more curious about Kennedy than about Roosevelt, more inspired by Charlie Parker than by Duke Ellington. She may be right, but I am more moved by Simone de Beauvoir's view that "every . . . death is an accident . . . and . . . an unjustifiable violation."

Steinem documents the unhappy childhood of Norma Jean Baker, "the real Marilyn Monroe" (44), and comes dangerously close to falling into the trap of advocating a traditional nuclear family as the precondition for emotional security and self-esteem, a position that Phyllis Schlafly and Jerry Falwell—and Dan Quayle—would find quite congenial. It is one thing to point out the scars of a neglected childhood and sexual abuse, but it is quite another, in an era of single mothers and fathers, and lesbian and gay parenting, to reduce her relationships with men to a search "for the fathering—and perhaps the mothering—that she never had" (103). Steinem, advocating a return to family values?

And Steinem's villains, too, are predictable: Norman Mailer, for his disbelief and obsession with Marilyn;[5] Freud, for his views on female passivity; Joe DiMaggio, whose puritanism presumably prevented him from apprehending that Marilyn's nudity around the house was "non-sexual," not intended to be provocative, but merely a source of "comfort," an innocent "childhood habit" (141); and, "men who are old or powerful or fond of degrading women" with their preference for "the variety of lovemaking" that resulted in Marilyn spending "a great deal of time on my knees" (159).

In fact, Steinem's book invites comparison with Mailer's, both glossy, with texts which are primarily intended to supplement the numerous photographs, and, inevitably, both exploitative. Just as anti-pornography is often just as titillating as pornography, so a book about "the real Marilyn" appeals to the voyeur in us as much as the books about the mythical Marilyn.

One difference between Steinem and Mayne is that the former barely acknowledges what is axiomatic for the latter, namely, that "without voyeurism there would be no cinema" (15). (It seems clear that movies and TV are inherently voyeuristic, in a way in that theatre and radio, for example, are not. What is not clear is why it should be so.)

Steinem apparently admires Monroe's talent and is critical of the general perception of her screen persona as that of a dumb blonde. Here, I think her attempt at sympathy backfires. Consider two of the films cited by Steinem in this connection, *The Seven Year Itch* and *Some Like it Hot*. In the first, according to Steinem, she is typecast as "the dumb-blonde-upstairs" and in the second, she plays "a blonde so out of it that she couldn't tell Tony Curtis and Jack Lemmon in drag from real women." Marilyn is quoted as saying, in connection with this latter film, "I've been dumb, but not that dumb."

But this simplistic analysis does a disservice to Monroe, and contributes nothing to our understanding of her appeal. In fact, a more careful reading of the films suggests something quite different. In *The Seven Year Itch*, Tom Ewell plays a husband and father whose family is gone for the summer. Monroe's openness and availability generate fantasies, but no more. In *Some Like It Hot*, Curtis is avoiding George Raft, who intends to kill him; hence the masquerade. In both cases, the men are obliged to suppress their sexuality in the presence of an over-whelmingly attractive woman. At least for the men in the audience, it is Ewell and Curtis who are dumb, not Monroe. In fact her anti-macho and anti-marriage comments to Ewell seem quite sensible. (Being married is like living in a ladies' club: "You have to be in by one o'clock every night.") In our fantasies, sex with Marilyn would be worth any risk, including loss of family and life. But she is doing more than feeding our fantasies. I suspect that Monroe is winking at us, simultaneously ridiculing and sympathizing with her society's repressed sexuality. And, indeed it is precisely this quality, I would maintain, that pro-vides one component of her political appeal.

Insofar as Monroe as victim is concerned, here, too, the situation is more complex. She was both more and less than a victim. She made it impossible for the generations of actresses and singers who followed her to have any illusions or miscon-ceptions about overt (what is sometimes mistakenly referred to as "innocent") sexuality. As Steinem points out, someone like Madonna, whose "symbols of femaleness are pure Marilyn," uses seduction "to get what she wants" (9).

Indeed, Monroe's role in the sixties is illuminated by the current debate about the role of Madonna's explicit sexuality. In the post-Monroe world of entertainment, no one seriously con-siders Madonna, or this month's Playmate, as victims. Rather the debate is whether or not Madonna is sexually liberating, in control of the representation of women's sexuality. I believe that precisely the same question ought to be raised about Monroe, in which case she might be seen as sexually emancipated, rather than sexually exploited. Conversely, it is a sad betrayal of the struggle for egalitarianism that a recent *Ms* had a feature story in which Cher, whose full-page ads for a chain of health salons suggest that her top priority is to get women to reduce their "butts" and "thighs"—is portrayed as a feminist idol. In today's feminism, there is hardly a distinction between profiteer and political activist.

And similarly with Marilyn as joke. I remember being in Brooklyn when Monroe's upcoming marriage to Arthur Miller

22

was announced. My friends and I laughed and joked, imagining what it would be like to introduce Marilyn Monroe as a prospective daughter-in-law to the stereotypical Jewish mother. But here, too, the joke was largely on us. On the one hand, we were Arthur Miller; but on the other hand, Miller was the incurably neurotic Portnoy, and Marilyn Monroe was his revenge. Consider the irony in someone marrying Marilyn Monroe, primarily as a way of getting even with his mother.

What do men want? The answer, at least in the case of Monroe, is not so obvious. I don't happen to share Mailer's view that what Marilyn offered was sex without danger or difficulty. Indeed, it is illuminating to compare, for example, the perceptions of three Spaniards, writer Terenci Moix, director José Luis Garci, and film critic César Santos Fontenia, whose articles about Monroe, in a recent edition of the Spanish weekly *ABC* (August 2, 1987) devoted to Monroe, on the twenty-fifth anniversary of her death, repeatedly make reference to their sense of "sin" and "guilt." Clearly any discussion of Marilyn Monroe will reflect, directly or indirectly, the author's views of sex. Sex has always had a dangerous, subversive component, all the rhetoric of the so-called sexual revolution to the contrary, notwithstanding. For my pre-AIDS generation, psychologically, the expression "safe sex" was always an oxymoron. Freud referred to romantic love as "a local psychosis"; Marx should have referred to it as "the opium of the masses." If Monroe "can be saved for feminism," it will be because she represents the genuinely revolutionary search for a third alternative in a society that seems to admit only of lust and sexual exploitation on the one hand, and some version of romantic love as the one conceivable, egalitarian alternative on the other.

Notes

1. Judith Mayne, "Feminist Film Theory and Women at the Movies," *Profession* 87 (1987): pp. 14–19.
2. Gloria Steinem, *Marilyn* (N.Y.: Holt, 1986).

3. The point has recently been made in a book by John Diggins, *The Rise and Fall of the American Left* (N.Y.: Norton, 1992), reviewed by Maurice Isserman in *The New York Times Book Review* (March 8, 1992): p. 9. "For Mr. Diggins, the influence that the academic left has attained within certain scholarly disciplines, particularly the study of literature, is less a reflection of its sinister power to warp young minds than of its headlong retreat from engagement with real politics." I take the humanities' recent infatuation with "theory" to be a symptom of this trivialization of political movements by academic scholarship. As Isserman quotes Diggins: "Since there is no world outside the text, the point is not to interpret the world but to capture the canon."
4. In contrast, see the allegations of Monroe's anti-Semitism made by Ted Jordan in *Norma Jean: My Secret Life with Marilyn Monroe* (N.Y.: NAL-Dutton, 1991).
5. Norman Mailer, *Marilyn* (N.Y: Grosset and Dunlap, 1973).

6

The Politics of Dirty Jokes: Woody Allen, Lenny Bruce, Andrew Dice Clay, Groucho Marx, and Clarence Thomas*

In one of Woody Allen's early movies, a woman asks him, "Does sex have to be dirty?" and the Allen character replies, "It does if you do it right."

Like most good jokes, this one is insightful as well as funny, or maybe it is funny because it is insightful. In any case, it addresses the inherent ambiguity of sex. The joke may be interpreted as puritanical: "sex is dirty," or, quite the reverse, it might be interpreted as libertarian: "dirty sex is (all)right."

A little refinement is required. Virtually no one, no matter how prudish, would admit to claiming that sex is always dirty (or sinful, or one of the other moral stigmas associated with it). Consider, for example, a recent syndicated column by James Kilpatrick (*Seattle Times*, August 25, 1991). It is a condemnation of what he considers today's sexual irresponsibility, and in it he expresses his distress at the fact that young people have converted "a sublime act between a man and a woman"—gays and lesbians, please note—into "a fun thing." So, the puritanical position is that responsible sex is sublime, and when it is fun, or *merely* fun, then it is morally suspect. Or, to translate the puritanical position into Allen's terms, if you're not doing it

*In press. Scheduled to be printed in *Humor* 7 (1994): pp. 173–75. Used with permission of Mouton de Gruyter, a division of Walter de Gruyter & Co.

25

right, in this case, within the context of a monogamous marriage, then it must be dirty.

I suppose that logically, there might be a third, libertine equivalent, which would be diametrically opposed to the puritanical one, whereby sex is the most fun when it is the dirtiest. Consider, for example, Lenny Bruce's contempt for the obscenity laws under which he was prosecuted for years: " . . . the literal view of the law is that what's obscene is *dirty* screwing and *fancy* screwing" (John Cohen, *The Essential Lenny Bruce*, p. 215, italics in the original), a view that he called "nonsense."

Bruce was quite explicit about his rejection of the whole concept of "dirty jokes." One of his bits dealt with "dirty toilet jokes," which he took to mean "jokes about dirty toilets": "*Look at you, you dirty, dopey, Commie toilet, you!*" (Cohen, p. 169). Bruce claimed that most "well" comedians (as opposed to the "sick" comedians) had given the word *motel* a dirty connotation.

Incidentally, on a recent talk show, Larry King was interviewing an attorney regarding the William Kennedy Smith rape trial, and the lawyer had made the point that one desirable consequence of televising the trial was that now, words like *penis* were being openly used. King agreed, and he added that Lenny Bruce had "died" for the right to use such words. But, in fact, Larry King misses the point about Bruce. I have read just about every routine that he did, and I cannot recollect him using the word *penis* even once, although there are innumerable references to *cocksuckers*. When ridiculing the Catholic church, he used outrageous euphemisms like "the genital apparatus," but his campaign was aimed at using the most emotionally charged taboo words, not the more or less clinical terms that have now found their way into the public media. If Bruce was, as his admirers claim, a martyr in the struggle for free speech, I am sure he would not consider the battle won.

The recent HBO special by Andrew Dice Clay generated a great deal of criticism, largely from groups that consider themselves politically progressive. However, it was not Clay's language that they objected to, but his politics. His line, "If you don't know the language, get the fuck out of the country," is offensive because it is jingoist not because it is a dirty joke. Andrew Dice Clay is to stand-up comedy what David Duke is to electoral politics, or perhaps, given Pat Buchanan's platform regarding immigration, he may be the Pat Buchanan of stand-up comedy.

I started this piece by claiming that a joke that was funny often was also insightful. It is a little disturbing to have to acknowledge that a joke that is funny may also be offensive, a view, incidentally, that some would like to exclude by definition, insisting that only jingoists can find jingoist jokes funny.

I have now referred to three quite separable but, I think, related, notions: humor, morality, and political ideology. The three converged in the recent televised hearings of Clarence Thomas's nomination, and Anita Hill's allegations of sexual harassment. The most publicized of Hill's allegations was that Thomas had made a joking reference to pubic hair, a reference that Hill had found particularly offensive. Interestingly, when asked by one of the senators whether, if true, the charges would constitute sexual harassment, Thomas immediately agreed that they would. It is of some significance that Hill, Thomas, the Judiciary Committee, and the media generally all agreed on one issue, namely, that telling offensive anecdotes in what quaintly used to be referred to as "mixed company" is not to be tolerated, at least in the workplace. Sexual harassment statutes consider such behavior illegal as well as immoral. In the movie, *Duck Soup*, Groucho Marx, as Rufus T. Firefly, the leader of Freedonia, sings his political platform: "Nobody's allowed to smoke; or tell a dirty joke." A case of art anticipating life?

Marx's joke is about dirty jokes, but no one could seriously argue that it is a dirty joke. Bruce may have told a lot of dirty jokes, but the one about the dirty toilet is presumably not one of them. Dice Clay's joke uses a dirty word and is politically offensive, but is hardly a dirty joke. Allen's joke refers to dirty sex. Does that automatically mean that it is a dirty joke? If so, we have legitimized a puritanical vision of society, which invites not only mass sexual repression, but a degree of censorship and intimidation that goes even further than that envisioned by the authors of the most restrictive obscenity laws.

PART II

LANGUAGE AND SOCIETY

7

Language in a Sexist Society*

A linguist trying to discuss language and sexism is immediately confronted with the absence of the relevant theory. First, we know very little of the relationship between language on the one hand and attitudes, beliefs and perceptions on the other hand. It is hard to demonstrate either that language determines or is determined by attitudes in spite of a tradition of heated discussion and exaggerated claims. For example, no one would seriously suggest that the substitution of *Black* for *Negro* either caused or resulted from the elimination or reduction of racism. Similarly, no conclusion can be drawn about sexist attitudes merely because *chairperson* increasingly replaces *chairman*. Rather it seems that language is to sexism as symptom is to disease. Fever doesn't cause flu, and flu doesn't cause fever; flu is presumably diagnosed on the basis of a set of symptoms of which fever is one; similarly with sexism and language.

Second, we know virtually nothing about how linguistic competence, that is, what speakers know about their language, interacts with beliefs and attitudes to determine linguistic performance, that is, how speakers use their knowledge. Thus, for most people, the sentence *My neighbor is a blond* is usually interpreted as referring to a woman although there is nothing

*A paper delivered at the December 1974 meeting in New York of the Modern Language Association, which also appeared in *Studies in Descriptive and Historical Linguistics* (1977): pp. 209–16. Reprinted with permission of John Benjamins Publishing Co., Amsterdam, Holland.

31

in the semantics of words for hair color to suggest that, when nominalized, they ought to refer exclusively to females. On the other hand, the fact that we talk about *unwed mothers*, but not normally about *unwed fathers*, is a linguistic observation that obviously is not unrelated to how society views parenthood and marriage. Neither language nor logic can account for the currency of one and not the other, since presumably they come in pairs.

In any case, the following facts of English and English usage provide data which presumably have to be accounted for by any general statements regarding the nature and function of sexist language in this society.

In English grammar, the masculine form is characterized as the unmarked category and the feminine as the marked. Thus, for example, there are a number of suffixes which explicitly refer to, that is, "mark" the feminine: *prince/princ-ess, wait-er/wait-r-ess, hero/hero-ine, comedi-an/comedi-enne.* Notice, however, that although *She is a comedian.* is acceptable, *He is a comedienne.* is not. Similarly, the marked form is often indicated by a pattern of modification, for example, *lady doctor* or *woman athlete*, opposed normally simply to *doctor* or *athlete*, not *man athlete*. This often results in anomalous constructions like *lady mailman* or *madame chairman*. Observe that in spite of the apparent contradiction an expression like *bachelor girl* is current, whereas *married bachelor* is semantic nonsense. Related forms of modification are illustrated by expressions like *career woman* on the one hand and *family man* on the other.

Another use of the unmarked form is its use to cover both categories, referred to as neutralization, as in the generic use of *man, mankind* and numerous expressions like *man-hours, man the boats*, even *oh, man!* But sometimes *man* is not used generically even though one might think it ought to be. *A man's home is his castle,* does not mean *A man or woman's home is his or her castle. Man* is not the only form used in this way; consider *brotherhood, fellowship, masterpiece* and *you guys*. Masculine pronouns are often used to refer to people of unknown sex, which explains the recent declaration by a self-righteous chairman that "we will hire the most qualified person regardless of his sex." Other languages have systems of grammatical gender which result in another form of neutralization. Spanish has *hermano* for 'brother' and *hermana* for 'sister' but *John and Mary are brother and sister.* is rendered by *Juan y María son hermanos.*

Perhaps just as revealing as the general case are the exceptions. English seems to have only one suffix marking the masculine, which occurs in the pair *widow/widower*. Examples where the masculine is expressed by a modifier include *male nurse, male model, male prostitute,* which seem to provide a comment on the activities expected of women. Interestingly enough, *male whore* and *male slut* are a little incongruous in most dialects. *Whore* and *slut* seem to have a moral connotation which seems somehow less central in *prostitute*, which seems to be primarily a statement about a person's source of income. There are cases where people of unknown sex are designated by feminine pronouns. Both pronouns were illustrated in an elementary school staff notice requesting that "the supervisor will make sure each of *his* teachers will fill out *her* forms." One area where the female is used to cover the entire species is in the words for certain animals, for example, *goose* in spite of the presence of *gander*.

Asymmetries are common in syntax; for example, one says *Widow Brown* but not *Widower Brown. Mary is John's widow* is obviously well-formed, but *John is Mary's widower* sounds a little strange. One can say *Mrs. John Smith* or *Mr. and Mrs. John Smith*, but not *Mr. Mary Smith,* or *Mr. and Mrs. Mary Smith*. The fact that *Mr.* and *Mrs.* are not equivalent is further illustrated by their conjunction with titles like *Dr.* and *Prof.* Thus, one says *Dr. and Mrs. Smith* if the doctor is male, but neither *Dr. and Mr. Smith* nor *Mr. and Dr. Smith* if the doctor is female.

Verbs for sexual intercourse are irregular in their syntax. Verbs like *screw* and *fuck* are asymmetrical compared to an expression like *to have intercourse with.* Both *He has intercourse with her* and *She has intercourse with him* are grammatical but

33

whereas *He screws her* and *He fucks her* are well-formed, *She screws him* and *She fucks him* are less clear. Indeed, the likely interpretation for the latter is metaphorical, where the verbs involve deception not sex. Parenthetically, that sex and deception should be semantically related is easier for women to explain than for linguists. The same process in reverse seems to be operating in expressions like *to do someone* and *to be had*. Conversely, an expression like *to put out* requires a feminine subject: *He puts out* seems strange. Not native to my dialect is the verb *to ball* which apparently is symmetrical in its syntax, allowing both masculine and feminine subjects. Conceivably the change in language is accompanying the change in attitude, as sex stops being something men do *to* women and something women do *for* men. However, for most speakers, *to ball* is sexist in its lexical associations. I am usually laughed at when I suggest that it might be associated with *to have a ball*.

Just as there is asymmetry in syntax, so there is asymmetry in the lexicon. For example, although *man* and *boy* may correspond to *woman* and *girl*, there is, at least in my dialect, no equivalent for *guy*. The words for males seem to provide for a general ageless category not available for females. Conversely, male *Mr.* corresponds to both *Mrs.* and *Miss*; here the words for females are over-differentiated. It is worth observing that both under-differentiation and over-differentiation are merely opposite sides of the same sexist coin. *Guy* is neutral as to age; *Mr.* is neutral as to marital state. Elsewhere in the vocabulary there are references to women with no male equivalent; consider for example, a word like *nymphomaniac*; in my dialect there is no parallel to *divorcée*; there is *housewife* but no *househusband*, and expressions like *old wives' tale* but no *old husbands' tale*. Quite apart from what one thinks of the institution, it is revealing that the activity is referred to as *wife-swapping* not *husband-swapping*.

Certain lexical fields have developed a proliferation of metaphorical terms, euphemisms and epithets. One such area is the words for women themselves. For example, they are referred to with words for food. Although *sugar* and *honey* are used to refer to both men and women, only a woman is normally referred to as *a dish* or *a tomato*. The word *peach*, incidentally, has become generalized so that it occurs in expressions like *a peach of a day, a peach of a movie*, etc.

Animal names are used metaphorically to refer to humans, and it is simplistic to claim that all such metaphors are offensive. A reference to a brave person as lion-hearted is surely not derogatory. But *chick, bunny, pussycat*, presumably refer to a soft, cuddly, petlike quality, *quail* is something that one hunts, and I don't know what the use of *barracuda* is supposed to mean. An explicitly sexual and sexist perception of women is illustrated by the fact that they and not men can be referred to as a *piece, piece of ass, piece of tail*. The word *lady* is more complex, involving distinctions of class as well as sex.

Exclusively female activities like pregnancy and menstruation have numerous euphemisms as well as epithets, *to be expecting* alongside of *to be knocked up, to be unwell* alongside of *to have the rag on*. On the other hand, activities like masturbation and intercourse are referred to as though they were exclusively male. Expressions like *to jerk off* invariably imply a penis or an ejaculation. The words for intercourse seem to combine elements of violence and contempt with eroticism. Football players anticipating sex report going home *to punish the old lady* and one novelist writing about a particular sub-culture uses the expression *to do the job on someone* both for sex and murder. Both the syntax of these words as well as their connotations suggest that sex is primarily a male-oriented activity. One cannot, for example, talk about a woman *plowing* a man. Not surprisingly, the euphemisms for sex, like *to sleep with someone* and *to go to bed with someone* are syntactically symmetrical.

That sex and violence are related is illustrated further by references to the penis with terms for tools or weapons. A sterile man, for example, is said *to be shooting blanks*. In contrast, one of the striking things about words for women's sexual organs is the absence of words for clitoris on the one hand and the proliferation of words for breasts on the other.

The unique perception of male sexuality is illustrated by current "hip" expressions like *to get off* with the meaning 'to enjoy' or *to get it up for something* with the meaning 'to be enthusiastic,' which presumably are semantic extensions of terms originally referring to male orgasm and to erection. And what can one make of the fact that fundamental ideas are referred to as *seminal*?

Certain areas of the vocabulary show similarity in form, but quite different meanings. A *governor* governs a state, but a *governess* governs children. A *mistress* is not a female mister. Similarly a *majorette* is not a woman major, nor is a *starlet* a woman star. In fact a *starlet* is not a star at all. A *laundryman* is usually someone who drives a truck and works for an established firm. A *laundrywoman* works for herself and delivers laundry in a basket. Some words apply to both men and women, but with different meanings. *He is a tramp* is a statement about finances; *She is a tramp* is about morals. In Spanish *El es inocente* means 'He is innocent,' but *Ella es inocente* has the additional meaning 'She is a virgin.'

Linguistic usage, what is sometimes referred to as pragmatics as opposed to syntax and semantics, is an area where language and attitudes interact by definition. Thus, for example, words like *promiscuous*, or *tease* in the sexual sense, are normally used to apply to women. Verbs like *titter, chatter, cackle* usually refer to women and/or children. The word *co-ed*, is used differently in *The school is co-ed* and *The school has co-eds*. Conversely, although words like *lawyer* and *doctor* are linguistically just as neutral as *friend* or *cousin*, they are perceived as referring to males, so that a group may be referred to as *lawyers and their wives*, and a caption in a history book can refer to *pioneers and their wives*. Similarly, a reference to a last name only is perceived as referring to a mate. A colleague reports writing an article with references to *Scott, Thackeray and Austen*, all of which were edited to read *Scott, Thackeray and Jane Austen*.

Sexuality is the basis of interpretation of a word like *couple* which is understood to be heterosexual, whereas a word like *cocksucker* is understood to be homosexual. It is surely not accidental that of the two, only the latter is used as an insult.

Finally, there are areas of the vocabulary which seem to be equivalent, but are ultimately asymmetrical. Thus, one hears *He bitches,* and *She bitches*, with the meaning 'complain,' and *He is an old maid* alongside *She is an old maid*, but the former member of each pair is to be understood as applying to men an undesirable quality usually associated with women. Conversely, a recent magazine article referred to Germaine Greer as a *ballsy feminist*. Thus, when men are cranky, they are behaving like women; when women are courageous, they are behaving like men. In this connection, to refer to, say, a difficult exam, as a *ball-buster* must be of limited significance to a woman. *Bachelor* and *spinster* are far from equivalent. One can talk of an *attractive bachelor*, but hardly of an *attractive spinster. Bachelor father* is a common expression usually referring, incidentally, to a divorced father, but *bachelor mother* is rare, and *spinster mother* is incongruous. The verbs *to father* and *to mother* have different meanings: *to father a child* is to be the biological father; *to mother a child* is to protect, perhaps over-protect it. Even *bride* and *groom* are not equivalent. One talks about *his bride*, but not of *her groom*. Indeed, a woman remains a bride for some undefined time, but a man stops being a groom the day after the wedding. Something about the relationship is reflected in the inclusion in the ceremony of the statement *You may kiss the bride* and not *You may kiss the groom.*

Probably the two most emotionally charged words in English are *cunt* and *prick*, particularly when applied to people. Again the use of a word for a part to refer to the whole person is not automatically objectionable. To refer to a compassionate person as being *all heart* or to an intelligent person as *a brain* seems anything but perjorative. However, in the case of the epithet for male genitals, the word seems to have little sexual connotation, often being merely a comment on the man's intelligence, whereas, in the case of women, the reverse is the case; *cunt* seems to imply a judgment about sexuality and morality.

One last, well-publicized example may illustrate how addi-

37

tional meanings are assigned expressions when they are applied to women. Consider the airline company slogan *We really move our tail for you.* For men, the slogan is two-ways ambiguous, referring either to the tail of the plane, or to the figurative meaning 'to work hard.' For women, the slogan is three-ways ambiguous, where the additional reading is the one where *move* is to be interpreted literally. The preoccupation with this part of women's bodies is not unique; in Seattle, a new women's clothing store is called Bottom's; the sign announcing the opening read, *Now, girls have Bottom's.*

I have provided relatively little in the way of explanation, and, I have even less to say about the political and social implications, and the alternative strategies they suggest for change. Clearly, the examples are far from exhaustive, and they represent a wide range, not only in terms of the particular aspect of linguistic structure, but also in the extent to which the facts are at the level of awareness and hence acknowledged by the average speaker. The more institutionalized a particular phenomenon becomes, the less visible, and presumably, the more resistant it is to change. Thus, one might question the effectiveness of a suggestion that we eliminate the word *seminar* because it shares the stem of the word *semen*, and undoubtedly was sexist in its origin.

Given the data, then, one can ask, is language sexist or are people sexist or is society sexist? The probable answer, regrettably, is all three.

8

Linguistic Taboos, Code-Words, and Women's Use of Sexist Language*

One of the privileges men enjoy in a sexist society is the greater latitude in the use of emotionally charged words. This inequity presumably is merely one example of a general situation, namely the demands on women to accede to norms of propriety.

Contemporary women, struggling to achieve a more egalitarian society, have resisted this asymmetry, and hence, one is now more likely to hear women use an expletive like *shit* in lieu of less forceful—what Lakoff[1] has called 'trivializing'—forms like *Oh dear* and *goodness*. However, many of these emotionally loaded words are themselves sexist. Hence, the double bind: either women refrain from using such expressions, thereby legitimizing men's privilege, or they do not refrain from using them, and thereby participate in their own degradation. The result is the incongruous situation whereby women who are indignant at the use of a word like *chairman* have nevertheless 'reclaimed' the word *bitch*. A related issue is the struggle to influence men in their linguistic usage, the current debate about pornography being essentially the logical extension of this position.[2]

The presence of a taboo word typically results in a proliferation of synonymous expressions, both euphemisms and emo-

*Originally published in *Maledicta* (1988–89): pp. 163–66. Reprinted with permission of Maledicta Press.

tionally charged words. So, for example, in certain segments of our society, the word *die* is avoided, being replaced by euphemisms like *to pass away* or *to go home*. Not surprisingly, there also exist frivolous or irreverent synonyms like *to croak* or *to kick the bucket*.

Similarly, then, for words referring to sex the euphemisms are expressions like *to sleep with someone* or *to go to bed with someone* alongside epithets like *fuck*. Incidentally, the euphemisms, but not the epithets, tend to have symmetrical syntax: *He sleeps with her; She sleeps with him*, whereas *fuck* tends to occur with a male as grammatical subject.[3]

Another linguistic device available in lieu of the taboo words is the use of 'code-words.' One common type of code-word is a word phonetically similar to the taboo word, e.g., *shoot* for *shit*, *fudge* for *fuck*. Paradoxically, the code-word can be substituted only for the expletive use, not the literal use of the taboo words. Thus *Oh shoot!* but not *I have to take a shoot*.

The use of phonetically similar code-words is not limited to English. Spanish speakers often use *miércoles* 'Wednesday' for *mierda* 'shit' and even the contrived *mi hermosa patria* 'my beautiful fatherland.'

The code-word may be a phonetically similar nonsense syllable: *frig* for *fuck, heck* for *hell*.

The code-word may be one part of a compound: *mother* for *mother-fucker; sucker* for *cocksucker*. Or the code-word may be an abbreviation: *s.o.b.* for *son of a bitch*. Even relatively innocuous terms are sometimes abbreviated, as in *b.m.* for *bowel movement* or *v.d.* for *venereal disease*, which seem to be abbreviations of expressions which are themselves euphemisms.

Occasionally, the code-word is completely arbitrary, as in the use in 'nursery' language of the expressions *number one* and *number two* for bodily functions.

A particularly insightful (and inciteful) use of a code-word was Lenny Bruce's recorded comedy routine, called "Blah Blah Blah." Bruce had apparently been arrested the previous evening during a performance at a club for having used the word *cocksucker*. He then reported on his appearance before the judge, and in order to avoid being arrested again, advised the audience that he would not repeat the word, "a ten-letter word, beginning with *c* and ending with *r*." In the course of the monologue, Bruce points out, first that the judge and police officers "like to say blah-blah-blah," and also, that the meaning of the word does not limit its use to male homosexuals, as the police imply, that is, the word is sexist in a rather unique way. What we have here, is a kind of word-magic, in which one use of the taboo word results in incarceration, whereas repeated use of the code-word is absolutely innocuous.

To make certain obvious distinctions explicit: not all taboo words are sexist: *bitch* presumably is; *shit* is not. There is a difference between a taboo word and a taboo act. Incest is a taboo act; the word *incest* is not a taboo word; the word *mother-fucker* is.

There are, then, three issues; first, the nature of linguistic taboos, which are not limited to, but often are sexual in their reference, and sexist in their usage. Consider uniquely female activities like pregnancy and menstruation. In addition to expressions like *to be expecting* and *to be unwell* one finds *to be knocked up* and *to have the rag on.*

Second, women and men may differ in their choice of expressions. If women tend to be more 'proper,' they are more likely to use more innocuous terms, euphemisms and code-words.

Third, the emotionally charged words, in contrast to the euphemisms, tend to be sexist, both in their assymetrical syntax and in their distinctive connotations: calling a woman a *cunt* is not the same as calling a man a *prick*, the former having much stronger sexual and moral connotations than the latter.

Now, the political strategy suggested by these observations remains an open question. Bruce is almost explicit in claiming that the existence of taboo words is itself pathological, and that repeated use of a taboo word will eventually defuse it of its emotional charge, a consequence he clearly considers desirable. This is a position that is shared by many contemporary young people who consider themselves progressive. But breaking a taboo is not the same as eliminating it. Given the fact that taboo

41

words persist, women seem to be in a double bind, because the two desirable consequences are mutually exclusive. They cannot simultaneously deny men their linguistic privilege and refrain from using sexist language.

The pornography issue can now be rephrased: Can a sexist society sustain an erotic language (or literature or art) which is not sexist?

Notes

1. Robin Lakoff, *Language and Woman's Place* (N.Y.: Harper & Row, 1975), p. 10.
2. Consider the form *cuntionary*, introduced presumably as a feminist alternative to a *dictionary*. The political effectiveness is not measured by the linguistic ingenuity.

    The dilemma that women face is not unlike the situation confronting blacks who speak a stigmatized dialect of English. Learning the prestige dialect, what is usually referred to as bidialectalism, is, in effect, legitimizing the bias of a racist class-conscious society. Refusing to learn the prestige dialect has obvious social and economic consequences.
3. The semantic and syntactic analysis of *fuck* is unclear. Specifically, whether the feature of 'penetration' is critical is open to debate, precisely because of the use of the word with a female subject. The issue may be clarified by considering an analogous case. The fact that one can say "She's one of the boys" does not invalidate that the word *boy* includes the feature 'male.'

9

Language, Sports, and Society*

The social function of sports has always been a topic of some interest, with proposals ranging from the suggestion that they serve to provide a sense of community to otherwise isolated individuals, to the analysis which condemns sports as little more than an opiate of the masses. That sports have always had social and political implications is obvious, and the appeal to "keep politics out of sports" is generally perceived to be vacuous rhetoric.

Within sports the race-track holds a unique position. It is generally understood that a race-track represents the intersection of gambling on the one hand and sports on the other. As a legalized form of gambling, betting on the horses, because of the potential for abuse and addiction, invites comparison to other social phenomena, both legalized and criminalized, like drinking, prostitution, and drugs. As an athletic event, it is comparable to other spectator sports like baseball or tennis.

Secondarily, both types of activities, the socially controversial ones on the one hand, and the athletic events on the other are businesses, with their consumers, entrepreneurs, victims, and beneficiaries. I omit here discussion of whether the transformation of, say, a football team into a business enterprise is a perversion or corruption of some noble ideal, or rather an inevi-

*Originally published in *Language in Society* 19 (1990): pp. 145–46. Reprinted with permission of Cambridge University Press.

table, predictable consequence, given the realities of our capitalist society. Betting on the horses has this special status; it is simultaneously socially suspect, while being an athletic event, and a business as well, and as such seems to provide an unusual microcosm of society as a whole.

Anyone interested in language would not be surprised to observe that the vocabulary of sports interacts in different ways with the social and political context. So, for example, sports terms become the metaphors for all kinds of everyday events and activities. And conversely, the language of sports reflects certain social values and norms.

Horse racing now provides the accepted vocabulary for political campaigns. The campaign itself is referred to as a 'race,' the leading candidate is said to be 'the front-runner,' other candidates are 'long-shots' or 'dark horses,' and the end of the campaign is the 'home stretch.'

Baseball terms are typically used as metaphors in a variety of areas. The introduction of a new variable results in 'a whole new ballgame.' In business and elsewhere, an acceptable offer is 'in the ballpark,' to make contact is to 'touch base,' to speak on someone's behalf is 'to go to bat' for them, the highest level is 'the big leagues,' as opposed to the 'bush leagues,' something unexpected is 'a curve,' questions are said to be 'fielded,' to mean business is to 'play hardball,' to take a turn is 'to have one's inning,' a list of participants is a 'line-up,' to take someone's place is to 'pinch-hit,' a running commentary is a 'play-by-play,' to postpone an invitation is to offer a 'rain-check,' to make some initial progress is 'to get to first base,' and to succeed, interestingly enough both with women and with drugs is to 'score,' while to fail is 'to strike out.'[1]

A similar list of metaphors can be derived from other sports. To be unfair is to 'hit below the belt,' and to give up is 'to throw in the towel.' (boxing); a person interacting with another is 'one-on-one,' (basketball); to deceive someone is to 'fake someone out,' an issue that politicians debate is a 'political football,' to begin something is to 'kick off' and someone who criticizes with

44

the benefit of hindsight is a 'Monday morning quarterback' (football).

But the language of sports consists of more than merely colorful metaphors assimilated into everyday usage. Racism and sexism both are manifested in the vocabulary of athletics. For example, teams still use the native American as mascot, with names like the Cleveland Indians and the Washington Redskins. In order to understand how offensive such terms are, think what the reaction would be to teams called the Kansas City Catholics, or the Minnesota Swedes, or the Detroit Negroes. Or, consider the fact that a short or 'cheap' homerun is referred to as a 'Chinese homer.'

In spite of the recent increased visibility of women in athletics, the language of sports is notoriously sexist: women basketball players still use a 'man-to-man' defense.

The race-track again provides an illuminating illustration of the assimilation of sexist values into sports. Horses that have never won a race, regardless of sex, are said to be 'maidens,' races for such horses are 'maiden races,' and a horse that wins for the first time is said to 'break its maiden,' an explicitly sexual and sexist metaphor. And the reverse process is equally common: horse terms are applied to women. A woman is referred to as a 'filly,' a heavy woman may be said to be 'packing a few pounds over,' the term used to refer to overweight jockeys. And a man in the company of an attractive woman is sometimes referred to as 'moving up in class,' a reference to the classification of race horses.

Thus, language suggests that the interaction between sports and society is in both directions. Sports both reflects and influences our social institutions, not often to the credit of either.

Note

1. Many of the above are listed in Tim Considine's *The Language of Sport* (N.Y.: Facts on File, 1982).

10

Old Maid and *Dirty Old Man*: The Language of Ageism*

It has often been noted (e.g., Lakoff 1975,[1] Saporta 1988[2]) that euphemisms and demeaning epithets tend to co-occur, as synonyms for linguistic taboos. The words to be avoided vary in reference, as well as the degree to which they are perceived as offensive. For example, for some speakers *to die* is a taboo word, replaced by a euphemism like *to pass away*, which co-exists with a word like *to croak*. Or, for the taboo word *pregnant*, one finds *to be expecting*, as well as *to be knocked up*. And, similarly for ethnic or racial groups: to the extent that *Jew* may be a taboo word, we find *anti-Semitic* as a euphemism for *anti-Jewish* alongside an epithet like *kike*.

It is my impression that the recent past has seen the increased usage of expressions like *senior citizens* instead of *old people* and *the golden years* instead of *old age*. The significance of such euphemisms should be obvious: old people are at best a source of fear and embarrassment, and at worst the object of contempt. (Compulsory retirement, for example, is nothing less than a form of bigotry.)

Derogatory expressions exist as well: *old bag, old fart, (old) fogey, (old) fossil, old goat,* and *(old) hag*, and there are insulting

*Originally published in *American Speech*, Fall 1991 (Vol. 66, #3). Reprinted with permission of the University of Alabama Press..

metaphors for people 'past their prime': *dead wood* or *over the hill.*

Part of the stereotype of old people is reflected in the use of words like *crotchety* and *bitter*; the latter suggests that their criticism or pessimism is exaggerated and unwarranted, and hence can be dismissed, not taken seriously. There are, of course, insulting expressions for young people, e.g., *little snot,* etc. However, the presence of such terms should not be taken to reflect some genuine egalitarianism.

Of special interest, since they reflect the interaction of sexism and ageism, are the expressions *old maid* and *dirty old man*, which are particularly illuminating when considered together; an old woman is ridiculed if she is not sexually active; an old man is condemned if he is. I have heard the derivative expressions *dirty old woman* and *dirty young man,* used frivolously; I don't recall ever hearing of a *dirty young woman* with a comparable connotation. Somewhat similar considerations apply to the expression *old lecher*.

The sexuality of the old, and of the very young, seems to be particularly disconcerting to our society. I have no doubt that the preoccupation with teenage pregnancy is in part a hypocritical disguise for the society's discomfort over the sexuality of teenagers. Public display of sexually based affection is a privilege reserved for heterosexuals, of the same race, provided they are neither too young nor too old. It also helps if they are physically attractive. Linguistically, in English at least, the bias against old people more closely resembles that towards racial and ethnic minorities, than it does the bias towards women. The latter is not only reflected in the lexicon, but in the grammar as well (suffixation, patterns of agreement).

One last point: we have all now learned not to refer to handicapped people as *cripples*. But the fact that we have created euphemisms like *disabled* or, incredibly, *differently abled* or *physically challenged* should not be confused with respect or acceptance.

Notes

1. Robin Lakoff, *Language and Woman's Place* (N.Y.: 1975).
2. Sol Saporta, "Linguistic Taboos, Code-Words and Women's Use of Sexist Language: A Double Bind," *Maledicta* 10 (1988): pp. 163–66.

11

Legally Married: Redundancy or Oxymoron?

For reasons that were personally compelling but academically irrelevant, I recently had cause to examine the meaning of the expression 'legally married.'

My old dictionary (Webster's Universal, 1936) provides the following definition for *marriage*: "The legal union of a man and woman for life," which is of interest in itself, since it seems to confuse both descriptive conditions ("legal union of a man and woman") and prescriptive conditions ("for life"); the last phrase has been deleted in more recent dictionaries (e.g., American Heritage, 1983).

My interest is linguistic, not legal, and I will therefore ignore the fact that there are differences in the laws regarding marriage from country to country and from state to state within this country. For that matter, I have to admit my confusion over the expression *common-law marriage*, defined as "a marriage by mutual agreement of the parties without formal ceremony, and provable by their subsequent conduct, such as living together as man and wife, acknowledging their relation before others . . . " (American Heritage). Are such couples *legally married?* In other words, there must be a law that defines the limits of common-law marriage. I assume, for example, that siblings, homosexuals, and children are prohibited from common-law marriage, just as they are prevented from being "legally married." If I am right, only the law can recognize a "common-law marriage," which, as far as I can see, makes it hard to distinguish from any other "legal marriage."

49

Current debates over whether gay and lesbian couples should be entitled to certain benefits and privileges reserved for heterosexuals is clearly a legal battle. Such couples who participate in "marriage ceremonies" presumably are not *married* because they are not *legally married*.

Or, consider the case of the bigamist (in a state where bigamy is prohibited by law). I assume that it is technically incorrect to refer to such a person as *illegally married* (to the second party). Rather, such a person is *legally not married*.

So, if marriage is essentially a legal institution, then it follows that the expression *legally married* is redundant. To be married is to be legally married; those who are not legally married are not married. As a basis for comparison, consider the expressions *entitled to vote* and *legally entitled to vote*. I assume that someone may vote illegally (e.g., by claiming to be someone else), but one cannot be "illegally entitled to vote," since presumably it is the law alone that determines who is enfranchised and who is not. I am not speaking here of the ethical question of who *ought* to be entitled to vote. I happen to believe that the restriction that limits voters to people of age eighteen or over is capricious and arbitrary, and that children under eighteen *ought* to be entitled to vote, but they are not; that is, they are not *entitled to vote* because they are not *legally entitled to vote*.

Consider, now, the other extreme, an institution that is clearly recognized as "extra-legal," say, a baptism or a bar mitzvah. Presumably, one does not ascertain whether someone has been baptized by appeal to the law. (I take the expression *the laws of the church* to be a kind of metaphor.) We understand that such institutions are religious, not legal, and therefore the expression *legally baptized* would be nonsense. If there are societies where such expressions are not self-contradictory, then those expressions constitute an interesting barometer of the extent to which such societies are theocracies. One last example: There may be cases where legal and religious counterparts coexist. That is, the fact that there is an expression *legal holiday* (e.g., Independence Day) does not preclude there being a meaningful expression *religious holiday* (e.g., Yom Kippur). When the two expressions overlap (e.g., Good Friday), that too is evidence of the incomplete separation of church and state.

Clearly, then, our legal system sees being married as being more like being entitled to vote than it does to being baptized. In our society, then, the expression *legally married* is redundant. In some hypothetical society, with a clear separation of church and state, the expression would be an oxymoron.

12

A Note on Foreign Accents: Language and Bigotry

It is universally acknowledged, among linguists, at least, that within any speech community, certain dialects are stigmatized and others are prestigious, and that the basis for this perception is social and political, not linguistic. So some years ago, Sledd[1] pointed out, in connection with black English, that members of our society "dislike black faces but use black English as an excuse," and that teachers try to change the color of their students' vowels because they cannot change the color of their skins.

It should come as no surprise, therefore, to discover that a society's perception of a foreign accent should be determined in essentially the same way. So, for example, English spoken with a French accent is more likely to be characterized as the language of a "cultured foreigner" than, say, the English of a native speaker of Greek; although there is a long tradition of ridiculing virtually all foreign accents, in general, the foreign accents of fair, northern Europeans tend to be more highly valued than those of dark, southern Europeans, South Americans, Asians, and Africans.

Recent history provides a dramatic example of the process at work. A former secretary of agriculture was presumably asked to resign for telling a racist joke. However, prior to that, he was involved in a different, less publicized incident.

Earl Butz was asked for his reaction to the then pope's objections to the use of contraceptives as a form of birth control.

Butz reportedly responded, "He no play-a da game; he no make-a da rules."

Butz could have said, "If he doesn't play the game, he can't make the rules," but he didn't. Instead, he caricatured an Italian accent—the pope at the time was an Italian—by a few transparent linguistic devices: negation with no auxiliary, word-final vowels for verbs, and the substitution of a stop for a continuant.

But what is of interest here is the intended effect of the caricature, namely to portray the pope as inarticulate and ignorant and thereby to discredit his position. (Actually, the issue is a little more complex since the speaker presumably reflects Butz's position, not the pope's.) In any case, the "success" of the joke is predicated on a perception of Italians as uneducated and illiterate, a perception that is allegedly reflected in their variety of English. To extend Sledd's assessment: it is foreigners we don't like; we use a foreign accent as an excuse.

Note

1. James Sledd, "Bi-Dialectalism: The Linguistics of White Supremacy," *Language: Introductory Readings*, Virginia P. Clark, Paul A. Eschholz, Alfred F. Rosa, editors (N.Y.: St. Martin's, 1972), pp. 418–29.

PART III

THE UNIVERSITY

13

The Linguistic Vigilantes: The Politics of Language Instruction*

It has now become part of the common wisdom that our language is deteriorating, that the current generation of students in particular and people in general are less articulate, less precise, and less sensitive to the great instrument that is the English language.

Different kinds of evidence are adduced to demonstrate the validity of this proposition, ranging from scores on national tests to the jargon of political figures. Similarly, there are a variety of explanations for the alleged decay including the insidious effect of television and the 'lack of standards' tolerated and even produced by 'a permissive society.' The proponents of this position include popularizers like Edwin Newman and John Simon, as well as academics, who argue adamantly for stiffer entrance exams, more required courses, revised graduation requirements, etc.

Rarely mentioned in the debate is the political and social context which surrounds the issue and which in fact determines the nature of the discussion. Ultimately, the issue is superficially linguistic, but more critically, political.

Any understanding of the basis of these assessments must start by making certain distinctions within the class of linguistic

*Originally published in the *Washington English Journal* (Fall 1981): pp. 2–3. Reprinted with permission of the *Washington English Journal*.

phenomena themselves. First, are facts of grammar, that is, general syntactic principles. So, for example, a black child who says *he tired* is exhibiting a rule for the deletion of *be* which is, in principle, no different from grammatical rules which are manifested in natural languages everywhere. The stigma attached to this dialect is social and political, not logical or linguistic. Indeed, to try to argue these questions on logical or linguistic grounds is, in fact, capitulating to the irrational.

Second, are lexical facts. Purists are distressed that in current usage *disinterested* is used interchangeably with *uninterested*. There are two points here. One is the inevitability of linguistic change. The attempts to resist change would be quaint and innocuous if it were not for the damaging consequences involved. The meanings of words change; the 'original' meaning has no privileged status. The fact that the word *breakfast* originally meant to *break a fast* does not suggest that we are misusing the word if we do not attach to it some religious connotation. The other point involved here is the relation of language to conceptualization. People who blur the distinction between *disinterested* and *uninterested*, so the argument goes, are fuzzy thinkers, incapable of subtle and precise discriminations. But what evidence is there for such a conclusion? Only the circular reasoning according to which clear thinking is illustrated by people who use *disinterested* with its original meaning. In fact, the gap in vocabulary that is left is readily filled by any of a number of synonyms. People who use *disinterested* where others use *uninterested* will learn to use *impartial* or *unbiased* where others use *disinterested*. There is no conceptual issue here.

A third type of evidence offered by the linguistic vigilantes is the use of language to obscure rather than to illuminate. This criticism is less clear because it is not at all obvious what is at stake. A characteristic example is that of a former presidential press secretary who, when confronted with an obvious contradiction between press releases, acknowledged that his previous statement was now 'inoperative.' Now there is certainly something reprehensible in an official representative of the government lying to the press. But that is a moral question, not a linguistic one. Dishonesty and mystification in government (or in advertising) should be relentlessly exposed, but we should not confuse our leaders' acts with the words they choose to describe those acts. An unprovoked military attack is no more or less acceptable because it is referred to as a 'preventive action.' Lying is the limiting case where the reprehensible act itself takes a linguistic form. In short, it is not our language which has deteriorated, but our integrity and sense of outrage.

Arguments such as mine have sometimes been misunderstood to imply that what is being defended is everything up to and including sheer incoherence, that what is being advocated is 'linguistic chaos.' No one with even a minimal awareness of the nature of language would sustain such a position. What characterizes language is precisely the tension between freedom and rules, that is, creativity within constraints. No one seriously maintains that 'anything goes.' But, by the same token, there is no basis for ascribing some intrinsic worth to one set of rules over another. The fact is that speakers of some dialects are stigmatized essentially because of their race and class; dialect differences are a rationalization, not a rationale. None of this is news to linguists. What is interesting is how insistently proposals are made and policies developed in which these facts are ignored, denied, and distorted.

But there remains one set of issues that is not addressed by the above. People, whatever their dialect, still should be encouraged to develop certain language abilities, like reading and speaking coherently and persuasively. I do not claim to know how to teach reading, and to the extent that reading involves the application of a rather complex set of principles, I doubt that anyone knows how to teach these principles. But, here too, there is a moralistic tone to the debate, which seems to me misguided. A friend of mine used to be a teacher in the roughest schools in New York. Her classes were referred to as the 'last stop before jail.' She used to begin her class by saying, "I'm supposed to teach you to read. But let's get one thing straight. Hitler knew how to read, and my grandmother didn't; but I'll still take my grand-

59

mother anytime." This is not a defense of illiteracy. But it is a justified attack on the pious equation of literacy and morality.

Higher education has its own cadre of purists among faculty and administrators. So, the perennial debates at the University of Washington regarding raised admission requirements for minority students obscure one fundamental aspect of the issue: any test which purports to determine students' ability to use the high-prestige dialect of English is likely to penalize students who speak a low-prestige dialect. There is nothing mysterious here. The effect of such tests is to deny admission to people on the basis of a criterion which is intellectually irrelevant, namely the dialect of English they speak. (There is a related issue hidden here, namely, the responsibility of a state institution to help identify and meet the legitimate intellectual needs of all the people.)

Given the current political climate, we can be sure that the vigilantes will be increasingly vocal. Their passion should not be allowed to obscure their lack of intellectual substance.

14

Professors Must Share the Blame for the Humanities' Decline*

Our Lack of Integrity and Principle Can Only Be Called Scandalous

In the continuing debate on the decline of the humanities, we typically blame such factors as the prestige and success of science and technology; the pernicious effects of television and pop culture: the restructuring of priorities because of limited resources; and the lack of preparation, curiosity, and intellectual talent of the new generation of students.

How about us—the professors of literature and art and history, the so-called humanists? I think we are much more culprit than victim, and should take our share of the blame.

As an example of the degree of our complicity, consider the typical procedures at large state universities when it comes time to determine salary increases. Such discussions invariably bring out the worst in faculty members.

Put a few bucks on the table, and scholars turn into scavengers. We become petty, self-serving, even greedy. As Robert Hutchins said when he was president of the University of Chicago, the reason university politics are so dirty is that the

*Originally published in *The Chronicle of Higher Education* 33, No. 4 (September 24, 1986): p. 80.

stakes are so low. Virtually none of us is immune; there are very few good losers, only good actors.

Recently the level of self-righteous indignation has been raised a notch at many universities, presumably because of a legislative mandate that salary increases be determined on the basis of "market demand." Much of this outrage seems hollow, if not downright hypocritical. It is and always has been common knowledge that the surest, most direct way to get a substantial raise in salary is to be in demand, to get a competitive offer—what in the National Basketball Association is called an offer sheet.

Paying people who are in demand more than those who are not is not news; what is now different is that it is explicit and, more interestingly, is accepted by university administrators and faculty representatives. But then I suppose that's not so surprising, particularly in institutions where a tradition of governance by administrative fiat is tolerated by an acquiescent faculty.

While this way of doing business may sometimes result in rewarding the deserving, it has also always served to encourage the opportunistic and the unscrupulous. Most of us have been pretty tolerant about the system, as long as it looked as though we might be the beneficiary—or at least not obviously the victim. So the current outcry about salaries is little more than the usual self-interest, now disguised as a defense of educational principle.

When someone insists that it's not the money but the principle, you can be pretty sure it's the money; or, more exactly, the ego, vanity, and false pride for which money is the barometer. This is particularly hard to take when one considers that tenured faculty members at large universities have virtually ideal working conditions.

We have maximum autonomy and mobility with minimum accountability and supervision; we are an extremely privileged segment of society, the prevailing myth to the contrary notwithstanding. Underpaid? Compared with what?

As another example of our complicity in the decline of the humanities, consider the interminable departmental discus-

sions about enrollment and jobs and the ability to place graduates—as though these constituted a reliable measure of the
intellectual vigor of a discipline. But the blurring of the distinction between the humanities and what might be called the
humanities business is not merely a poor choice of tactics; it
marks a fundamental capitulation on the part of scholars in the
humanities to the values of the marketplace—precisely those
values to which the humanities are presumably opposed.
There's an ad for the *Wall Street Journal* that says the paper
"has no business section—it's all business." Many of us feel the
same could unfortunately be said of the modern university.

What academe often refuses to recognize is that educational
values and marketplace values are not always complementary;
in fact, they are in significant ways contradictory. Imagine a
chairman of the board telling a meeting of stockholders that
there will be no dividend this year because of the company's
commitment to aesthetic and ethical principles. I'm sure you
can't.

It should be just as hard to imagine faculty members' being
told—as they are by legislators and college administrators—
that their salary levels will be based on the marketability of
their courses. This posture is not, as the legislators and administrators would have us believe, an innocuous compromise made
on the basis of expediency. It constitutes what in a less civil
subculture would be called a sell-out.

Anyone who has ever watched a TV commercial knows that
the marketplace tends to confuse visibility with worth and
thrives on the public's inability always to make the distinction.
So, by legitimizing the idea that teaching the humanities must
be justified in quantitative terms, we end up betraying ourselves
and our disciplines.

What are the figures on jobs and enrollment supposed to
demonstrate? Cervantes and Picasso, for example, do not need
our defense, and mediocre professors of Spanish literature and
art history do not deserve it. In equating them, we are ascribing
virtue by association. It won't work.

As we all know, debates about the relationship between

63

humanistic and scientific disciplines constitute a discipline of their own. But in recent discussions, intellectual questions of genuine interest have been trivialized to an embarrassing extent. Scholars in the humanities have always had a love-hate relationship with the sciences. On the one hand, the humanities are alleged to be the last repository of morality in a world dominated by scientists who in their insatiable search for the truth have sold their souls to the Devil; Frankenstein and Dr. Faustus are our adversaries. On the other, literature scholars (for example) often borrow the other side's terminology. They like to talk of "scientific" literary criticism or "theories" of poetry—remarkable pretensions in a discipline where many of the practitioners are often virtually incoherent when they try to provide relevant evidence to support a claim, and seem incapable of maintaining the distinction between assumptions and conclusions.

Finally, the complaint that the humanities are suffering because students are "unprepared" is strange coming from professors who claim to be devoted to developing their students' mental powers and to nourishing and passing on truths that are presumed to be universal. Are we to understand that the humanities no longer have anything to do with humanity?

The humanities may indeed be in trouble. If they are, it's not because of their adversaries; it's because of a lack of principle and integrity among their advocates. The humanities will thrive when they are no longer in the custody of educational mandarins but are restored to teachers who are intellectually honest and give substance to aesthetic and ethical values.

Of course there are plenty of people who maintain that those lofty principles have always been vacuous clichés, to be displayed when convenient and ignored otherwise. According to them, it is high time things were put on a more businesslike basis.

If they are right, then at least we can now be spared those sanctimonious pronouncements by university presidents and provosts and deans about collegiality and the community of scholars, and particularly that old thigh slapper about the critical importance of a liberal education in a free society.

15

The Use of Teaching Associates*

It is now commonplace for foreign language and English departments, particularly those at large state universities, to use (I
choose the word advisedly) part-time, temporary faculty to staff
our elementary or intermediate language courses. There are
slight variations, but in one common pattern, such persons teach
three times the load of graduate-student teaching assistants for
two times the salary. They receive virtually no benefits and have
no job security. It is not hyperbole to characterize their employment as exploitative. The fact that in hard economic times,
people will prefer unfair employment to no employment is
inadequate rationalization for such ethically questionable policies. That much is hardly controversial, and should, one would
think, constitute basis enough for discontinuing the practice;
but, it hasn't, and if the issues are seriously discussed at all, the
ethical issues are ignored, and the arguments are made on the
basis of programmatic needs. Cutting ethical corners is justified
on the basis of expediency and the alleged strengthening of the
program.

In fact, I think quite the opposite is the case. The use of
temporary, part-time faculty is short-sighted, detrimental and
ultimately counter-productive. The benefits are purely economic, and the costs are high both in human and intellectual
terms. Teaching associates function neither as students nor as

*Originally published in the *PMLA* (January 1988): pp. 63–64.

66

scholars, and as such are marginal and marginalized within the department and beyond. Rather than strengthening the program, their presence tends to weaken it, not because of the quality of instruction, which often is quite high, but because a language program staffed by second-class citizens tends to be isolated from the other components of the department ('ghettoized') rather than integrated with them. It is axiomatic that that part of the program which is in the custody of marginal faculty will be viewed as marginal. This arrangement merely legitimizes the view, already pervasive, that the primary function of a language department is utilitarian rather than humanistic, a form of capitulation, which in this case, borders on academic suicide.

In short, the use of teaching associates, rather than being an innocuous compromise, reflects quite directly on the educational and intellectual climate that produces them, and provides an interesting perspective on what is generally agreed to be the deterioration of the humanities.

It is usually assumed, without debate, that the difficulties facing foreign-language departments are largely due to a scarcity of resources, and as a corollary, that the remedy is largely financial. A look at the recent history of foreign-language instruction in this country suggests something quite different. The passage in the sixties of the NDEA provided funds for language fellowships, institutes, and foreign language teacher training. Foreign language instruction was never better funded. But the availability of money was, not surprisingly, a mixed blessing. The strings attached were quite severe. Language instruction was to serve a rather narrow utilitarian function, within the political context of the time. Language was in the service of business and government. This was quite explicit; for example, given the prevailing rationale, there could be no justification for the support of the classical languages, which by definition, were non-functional. Thus, language instruction was understood to emphasize the spoken language, communication was the primary goal of language instruction, and Russian and Chinese were suddenly discovered as neglected languages. The result was a rather sharp transformation in focus. Concern for truth, beauty, and virtue was replaced by the criterion of utility. And foreign-language departments saw themselves as the beneficiaries, not the victims. They had more students, more faculty, more degree programs. The humanities business was booming.

Now, fifteen or twenty years later, the fellowships and institutes are gone; what remains is the ideological residue. The rhetoric of aesthetic and ethical values seems hollow in the contemporary university with its concern for FTE's and SCH's. Language departments now have the worst of both worlds. We sold whatever was left of our humanistic soul to the marketplace devil, and now have the benefits of neither. Our colleagues in the classical languages were on the side of the angels. Whatever their faults and limitations, nobody ever thought that the purpose of Latin instruction was to enable the traveler to buy a toga.

The faculty in the humanities have traditionally been uniquely arrogant in our refusal to meet the most minimal demands of accountability. Anybody who questioned our legitimacy was a philistine, deserving only scorn and ridicule. Ironically, we now are required to justify what we do in the most anti-humanistic terms, succumbing to the cost-accounting mentality which completely dominates today's educational institutions.

Indeed, a comparison of the character of university faculty over the years is instructive. The previous generation was elitist, paternalistic, quite comfortable with the privilege of what was essentially a white, male province. Today's faculty member displays at least a veneer of egalitarianism ('Call me "Jack" '), but is more cynical and opportunistic than his or her predecessor, and is quite tolerant of an educational climate in which what matters are national rankings, outside offers, visibility rather than substance, and economic viability. While still preaching the value of the traditional humanistic virtues, we carry on our daily affairs according to the law of supply and demand. These are the faculty who campaigned shamelessly for increasing foreign-language requirements, without any concern for how the additional classes were to be staffed. Under those circumstances, there is nothing more natural than a kind of academic colonialism, in which elementary language classes provide the statistical rationale for the exercise of personal ambition by tenure-track faculty, whose opinion of their part-time colleagues and the function they perform is very close to contempt.

Rather than being an innocent solution to a temporary emergency, the hiring of teaching associates turns out to be a rather reliable litmus test of the intellectual vigor and sincerity of the modern-day language department. Find a modern language or English department where elementary and intermediate language instruction is primarily in the hands of temporary faculty, and you are likely to find a department that is morally unprincipled, and not surprisingly, intellectually stagnant. Rather than being a minor contradiction, this predatory use of cheap labor is symptomatic of a fundamental hypocrisy and lack of integrity.

16

*Profscam**

Although there are relatively few references to linguists or linguistics in this book, the issues raised will be familiar and relevant to any actual or prospective academic.

The book is easy to read, and in a sense, it was easy to write. Not that Sykes hasn't done his homework; he has. But documenting the "demise of higher education" requires more than merely providing examples of poor teaching and vacuous research.

Sykes' contempt for the modern academic is undiluted: they are "mobile, self-interested, and without loyalty to institutions or the values of liberal education," not merely obscurantists, but politicians and entrepreneurs, who "have been remarkably successful in diverting attention from themselves and assigning blame elsewhere." (p. 7)

Some might find Sykes' bill of indictment of today's professor unduly harsh (although others of us might be inclined to add a few more charges):

"They are overpaid, grotesquely underworked.

"They have abandoned their teaching responsibilities and their students. To the average undergraduate, [they] are unapproachable, uncommunicative and unavailable.

"In pursuit of their own interests ... they have left the

*Originally published in *Anthropological Linguistics* 30 (1990): pp. 250–52. (Review of *Profscam* by Charles J. Sykes. Regency Gateway, Inc., 1988.)

nation's students in the care of an ill-trained, ill-paid, and bitter academic underclass.

"They have distorted university curriculums to accommodate their own narrow and selfish interests.

" . . . bad teaching goes unnoticed and unsanctioned, and good teaching is penalized.

"They have cloaked their scholarship in stupefying, inscrutable jargon. This conceals the fact that much of what passes for research is trivial and inane.

"They have twisted the ideals of academic freedom into a system in which they are accountable to no one, while they employ their own rigid methods of thought control to stamp out original thinkers and dissenters.

" . . . the professors' relentless drive for advancement . . . has turned the American universities into vast factories of junkthink . . . " (p. 5–7)

Obviously, Sykes has been around the academic block. Each charge is documented by illustrations that are both painful and laughable. So, for example, the preoccupation with national attention has led to the 'star system' whereby Jihan Sadat, Anwar Sadat's widow, was paid $314,000 for "a single course in Egyptian culture for three semesters." (p. 72)

Sykes' perspective is illustrated by his ridicule of James Sledd's anti-prescriptivist views regarding English teachers. Sledd has argued what is obvious to virtually any student of linguistics, namely, that there is a political rather than a linguistic basis to the English profession's insistence on teaching the prestige dialect, and furthermore that 'standard' English is a " 'tool and instrument' of the dominant used for domination.' " Sykes sees this as "ominous" and part of a "trend . . . toward mediocrity." (p. 93)

A friend of mine used to teach reading in the New York public schools. Her class was for those students who had repeatedly failed; the class was referred to as "the last class before jail." On the first day of class, she would tell the students, "I'm supposed to teach you how to read, but let's get one thing straight: Hitler knew how to read, and my grandmother didn't, but I'll take my grandmother anytime." The position of people like Sledd and my New York friend are not a defense of incoherence and illiteracy, but rather an attack on the tacit assumption of many, including Sykes, that there's a correlation between literacy or schooling and morality.

Linguistic students will be interested in the critical remarks about the use of foreign students as teaching assistants (p. 69), and how the primary function of T.A. money is to produce Ph.D.'s. Sykes is undoubtedly right that the quality of undergraduate instruction at state universities has been deteriorating, but it is hypocritical to single out teaching assistants, and bigotry to focus on foreign students. In Sykes' defense, the mediocre faculty teacher is not completely ignored.

So, although Sykes understands something of the privilege and comfort of today's academic, his remedy may be worse than the disease, his first proposal being the abolishment of tenure. Furthermore, all professors, in his view, should be required to teach at least three courses a quarter, proposals which would blur the distinction between higher education and high schools. Maybe that's a suggestion that is worth considering, but it's not obvious that it constitutes a cure for what is wrong with today's university.

Sykes never asks why such a system thrives, if in fact, the students, and ultimately, the society are being cheated as he suggests. So, for example, Sykes repeats the complaints of corporate America that today's college graduates are unprepared for the roles they are expected to assume in business and government. But these are surely crocodile tears. Universities could not exist if it weren't for the support of business and government; (the two are equivalent). Twenty years ago, there was an outcry when a corporate manager decreed that "what's good for General Motors is good for the country." Now, it is taken for granted that the corporate interest and the national interest are synonymous, and that the university's function is to help business and government to act in their own narrow interest. Therefore, in a system where education is increasingly replaced by certification, students are not the victims, but the beneficiaries. Mediocrity persists because of the elitist conspiracy between students and professors. The latter agree to certify the former; in return the students agree not to blow the whistle on the faculty. It is the rest of society that pays the price.

17

A Case of Sexual Harassment

I have recently undergone the most difficult period of my academic life due to a complaint filed against me alleging sexual harassment, which resulted in my forced retirement.

Under the circumstances I can hardly be dispassionate, and it goes without saying that for some the following will be dismissed as the rationalization of irresponsible behavior. In fact, sexual harassment, by its very nature, is one of those offenses, like racism, which is almost universally denied. Nevertheless, once the initial humiliation of the quasi-legal process began to erode, it became clear that the incident raises issues that warrant some consideration and debate.

University Politics: The Abuse of Power

One crucial element contributing to the findings of a faculty committee that sexual harassment did indeed take place is the "inherent power discrepancy between a professor and a student." The nature and function of this "power" seems to me to deserve some discussion.

That the relationship between faculty member and student is asymmetrical is obvious; that the asymmetry is inevitable is less clear. In an institution dedicated exclusively to education, authority would presumably be ascribed to an individual by virtue of that person's ideas, the extent to which they were coherent, persuasive, and compelling. In an institution, like the modern university, whose function is primarily that of certification, authority is determined by rank and position, a different matter altogether. One would hope that there might be some correlation between the two types of authority, but the counter-evidence is abundant.

Now, it is not surprising that the loudest voices arguing against the "abuse of power" turn out to be the same as those who defend most vigorously the need for maintaining the discrepancy, insisting, for example, in excluding students from genuine participation in the serious decision making that governs their education. Analogously, I suppose, there were undoubtedly plantation owners who argued vehemently for better treatment of the slaves, and then were equally adamant in opposing their emancipation. The most obvious, direct way to reduce the "abuse of power" is to redistribute that power more equitably. This was obvious to large segments of the anti-authoritarian student movement of the sixties, a movement that is now dismissed as "immature" and "misguided." Until the campaign to convert the university into a more democratic institution is revived, the indignation and self-righteousness about the abuse of power sounds hollow.

The matter is even more ambiguous when it deals with the power over former students. As a retired professor, I am now presumably free to approach former students with no fear of sanctions at all. I mention this not merely to be facetious, but to suggest that the relationship of a faculty member to a former student is anything but clear, and that under those circumstances, the insistence that there is still an "abuse of power" may not be very compelling.

The question of power is of considerable relevance in determining whether or not there has been sexual harassment, since it is generally agreed that behavior that would normally be viewed as innocuous between peers may be perceived as coercive and threatening when coming from a person in authority.

Compare the situation of faculty member to former student with a quite clear situation, namely that of a tenured faculty member to a nontenured faculty member in the same department, where quite explicitly the former votes on and helps determine the promotion and tenure of the latter. Although the potential for abuse is more dramatic, it is tacitly understood that faculty members will be able to resolve potential differences in much the same way that other adults do. But the university has a considerable interest in denying that college students are adults. (It might be interesting to speculate about what the university policy might be in the case where it is a student who expresses sexual interest in a faculty member.)

One has to consider the possibility, then, that although routinely denied, what is at issue is sex between faculty and students, as much as sexual harassment. And I think there is some legitimacy to this concern since frequent sexual relationships between students and faculty, and public knowledge thereof, could undoubtedly erode the fragile basis of the privilege and authority that the faculty currently enjoy.

There is in fact some evidence to support these speculations. One administrator at the University of Washington has been quoted as stating that the sexual harassment policy was not intended to prevent faculty and students from "falling in love." Another pointed out that there was no objection to faculty and students having relationships that ended in marriage. The conclusion is clear. The semi-official policy regarding faculty-student relationships is that sex is acceptable if it is accompanied by "love" or leads to marriage (or both). To characterize such a view as puritanical is charitable; it is, in fact, a form of sexual apartheid, which legitimizes and reinforces the socially established power relationships between sexual partners. A similar criticism was an essential component of the student movement of the sixties: "At Cal State, also, there is an unwritten law barring student-faculty lovemaking. Fortunately, this anti-miscegenation law, like its southern counterpart, is not 100 percent effective" (Jerry Farber, *The Student as Nigger*, New York, 1969, p. 90).

Indeed, at least as far as colleges and universities are concerned, the notion of "consenting adults" has, for all intents and purposes, been abandoned. In fact, the ombudsman at the University of Washington is quoted (*University of Washington*

Daily, January 7, 1992) as follows: "To me, the only consensual relationship is one between equals," from which it follows that the person highest in the university hierarchy ought to be celibate. Less facetiously, such a position implies that in all other relationships, there is, by definition, an element of coercion, a view that seems to me to be a rationalization for mass sexual repression. Add to this view, the one reported to me by more than one investigator, namely, that "the victim is entitled to define harassment."

Furthermore, that the holder of such views should be precisely the person responsible for the primary investigation into charges of sexual harassment, would, one would think, raise serious questions about the nature of the process for resolving such conflicts.

Some colleagues, in an attempt at support, suggested a petition, citing my years of teaching, helpfulness to students, etc. I discouraged such an effort and agreed completely with those who, with quite different motives, argued that such considerations were irrelevant. The petition I would like to have seen was one in which faculty members, both male and female, heterosexual and homosexual, acknowledged that they had had sexual relationships with students or, perhaps more to the point, that they had tried unsuccessfully to have such relationships, a petition that is unlikely to get circulated.

A discrepancy in power is not unique to the faculty-student relationship; in fact, it seems to be an integral feature of most relationships: the parent-child relationship, the husband-wife relationship, the employer-employee relationship, to name only the most obvious. In other words, the faculty-student relationship is, like every other, in some ways unique; that's a truism. But some of its features are universal. We have, I suspect, exaggerated the uniqueness in the faculty-student relationship and ignored what it shares with other relationships.[1]

Incidentally, my attempts to raise some of these issues during the initial stages of the investigation were dismissed as "intellectualizing," the irony of which will not be lost on critics of contemporary education.

Sexual Politics

How one views sexual harassment cannot be separated from one's sexual politics. Feminism comes in many varieties, but what feminists presumably share is a commitment toward a more egalitarian society. That men in the present society have privileges by virtue of their sex is axiomatic. To overstate the case a little, the libertarian proposal for narrowing the gap is to emancipate women; the puritanical alternative is to repress men. The extreme positions on an issue such as pornography illustrate the diametrically opposed alternatives.[2]

I do not wish to paint with too broad a brush, but I think it is an accurate generalization to characterize academic women during the last twenty years as having moved from an essentially libertarian position to a more puritanical one. Women in the sixties no longer aspired to be "good wives," nor did they aspire to be "good students," essentially for the same reasons: they viewed both institutions as more confining than fulfilling. The women who initiated women's study programs were the same women who staffed rape relief centers and picketed beauty contests. Not only the personal, but the professional, too, was political. On the other hand, too many of today's academic women have manufactured careers for themselves out of a professed "concern" for women, a concern that is little more than a sanctimonious camouflage for what I, at least, perceive to be their puritanical sexual politics. In short, they are more the beneficiaries of the women's movement than they are contributors to it. Interestingly, both academic women in general and misogynist men agree in characterizing the former as "feminist," but with quite different motives. Today's academic women insist on referring to themselves as "feminists," largely to derive the benefits of a tradition that has struggled valiantly to deny men undeserved and unwarranted privilege. And, conversely, they are denounced as "feminists" by the regressive element that strives to maintain that privilege by discrediting any movement that might constitute a challenge to their status.

And, obviously, assumptions about sexuality are an integral component of any feminist politics. When I recently asked a group of students to speculate on what they considered to be "healthy sexuality," they laughed. Someone suggested that the expression was an oxymoron and repeated the observation that men and women must have come from different monkeys. Nevertheless, all statutes and investigations of sexual harassment presuppose a set of assumptions about acceptable and unacceptable sexuality, assumptions that are rarely explored and that, to make my own bias explicit, I think are quite pernicious.

It should be obvious that the words we use to discuss sexual relationships are ideologically loaded. Merely consider expressions like *fidelity, couple, womanizer, casual sex, seduction, adultery, philanderer, prostitute*, and all the others. They are hardly politically neutral. Flirtation can be either frivolous and pleasant or threatening and ominous. For some, marriage is a sacred commitment; for others, it is a form of tyranny.[3]

So, consider the language of the faculty committee report in which the offending behavior is characterized as "repeated unwelcome sexual advances." The term *sexual advances* seems normally to have a hostile connotation that, say, the word *flirtation* does not usually have. Indeed, it is of some interest to examine the words that are typically used to refer to the early stages of a sexual relationship: *to come on, to make a pass, to hit on someone* have a cavalier connotation of insincerity, which, for example, *to ask for a date* does not. *Seduction* is morally questionable; *courtship* sounds absolutely Victorian. Perhaps the fact that there seems not to be a neutral expression for such behavior is related to its inherent ambiguity. Recent newspaper reports of well-publicized cases of sexual harassment have repeatedly used the expression "uninvited sexual advances." What is an *invited* sexual advance?

But more significantly, I think, is the observation that this behavior was "repeated." In fact, it was pointed out on numerous occasions by various persons involved in the investigation that it was particularly damaging for me to have expressed sexual interest in a number of different students. This could only mean that my motives were suspect, that there could be no genuine affection, that there was a "pattern," which was reprehensible by definition. The administrative metaphor of choice was that the complaints might represent the "tip of the iceberg." The assumption is quite clear: monogamous relationships are healthy; nonmonogamous relationships are morally questionable. Someone who questions the assumption will not be heard, and anyone who suggests that the reverse might be closer to the truth is considered pathological. This is not intended as hyperbole; had I not retired, I would have been obliged to seek "counselling."

Sex and Age

The university newspaper quoted one student as referring to me as "old enough to be my grandfather" (*University of Washington Daily*, May 29, 1990), reported with no further comment. Imagine, as a basis of comparison, a similar situation involving a black faculty member and a student saying something like, "He's as black as the ace of spades." The blatant racism would virtually discredit the complainant, providing rather persuasive evidence of a double standard. But, paradoxically, comparable bigotry toward old people is so prevalent that it is not even recognized. (My suggestions during the investigation that age discrepancy might be a relevant factor were systematically ignored.)

That there is a warped perspective in our society toward the sexuality of old people is manifested in a number of ways. Consider, for example, terms like *old maid* and *dirty old man*, of some interest because they demonstrate the interaction of sexism and ageism; an old woman is ridiculed if she is not sexually active, and an old man is condemned if he is. One of the privileges that young people enjoy is that of being able to express sexual affection in public withour sanctions. Such behavior is normally inoffensive if the people involved are of the same race, heterosexual, and young (but not too young; the preoccupation with teenage pregnancy is in a part a hypocritical disguise for the concern with teenage sexuality). It also helps if they are physically "attractive." We don't want to see fat people, or handicapped people, being too sexual. And we don't want to acknowledge the sexuality of old people either. The "dirty old man" stereotype is as deeply ingrained as it is insidious, and the university's version of the syndrome is the "dirty old professor." I am familiar with a number of professors of literature, for example, who have expressed increased self-consciousness when they teach erotic poetry because they sense that they are more likely to be perceived as lascivious as they get older. The old professor is more corrupt and, hence, more corrupting. (As an aside, one should note that the existence of a euphemism *senior faculty*, like its nonacademic counterpart *senior citizen*, constitutes linguistic evidence of a double standard; euphemisms tend to replace expressions that are avoided, often because of some emotional charge.)

An old (male) faculty member's sexual interest in a young (female) student is morally suspect, by definition. An interest in a number of students is absolutely unpardonable. Once those assumptions are understood, the results of any investigation are quite predictable.

The Resolution of Conflict

I am sure that it is in part unavoidable in cases of sexual harassment, but there was a voyeuristic tone to certain aspects of the investigation that I found a little demeaning. But, in part, I think my reaction was the result of the nature of the process itself. As far as I can determine, at most universities, the formal complaint is filed either with the Human Rights Office, or with the Equal Employment and Affirmative Action Office, which, at the University of Washington, claim to "protect the interests of all those involved." However, in spite of the fact that the office portrays itself as impartial investigators, it is clear that they also act as advocates for the complainants, sometimes, for example, cooperating in composing the written complaint. The fact that these two separate and necessary functions converge skews the process from the very beginning. In fact, the history of affirmative action and human rights in our universities makes it obvious that such offices must be staffed by advocates for women and minorities. It would be unconscionable for them to actually be "impartial"; but it is hypocritical for them to claim that they are.

But I think a more general issue emerges. In any society some persons will behave badly, irresponsibly, unethically. And a mechanism for the resolution of conflicts caused by such behavior is necessary.

I indicated at the outset that I found the investigative process humiliating. More than that, I found it isolating, alienating, Kafkaesque. Part of my reaction was undoubtedly a result of the particular nature of the charges, but I suspect that others have experienced similar feelings under different circumstances. It seems to be an almost inevitable consequence of the adversarial system that the rhetoric escalates, positions become hardened, and the emphasis is on each side attempting to discredit the other. Vindication and vindictiveness become surrogates for justice. I have to believe that there must be a more humane alternative. Equally important, is whether such a mechanism ever achieves the kind of empowerment of potential victims that is presumably one of its primary functions.[4]

One last, personal note. A friend observed that my experience was as close as one normally gets to attending one's own funeral. There's an element of truth there. I received numerous expressions of affection and concern, which were a source of considerable comfort. Those people are my colleagues in every sense, and my gratitude towards them is deep and lasting.

But, conversely, it has been disheartening to have to acknowledge that not all co-workers are colleagues. Quite apart from the legitimate political differences, there are those who are judgmental, sanctimonious, opportunistic, and completely unprincipled, politically doctrinaire, "knee-jerk" feminists. When someone insists that they are trying to be "fair to both sides," the chances are that they are equally indifferent to both sides. The pervasiveness of such hypocrisy in our institutions of higher education, as in the rest of society, should, one would think, be a matter of general concern.

Notes

1. The following anecdote, told by a psychoanalyst and reported by Janet Malcolm in *Psychoanalysis: The Impossible Profession* (N.Y.: Random House, 1982), p. 76, regarding the nature of psychoanalysis may be illuminating in this regard:

   "I remember a seminar I once attended that was led by a brilliant and flamboyant Hungarian analyst named Robert Bak. The issue under debate was the nature of transference, and I raised my hand and asked rhetorically, 'What would you call an interpersonal relationship where infantile wishes, and defenses against those wishes, get expressed in such a way that the persons within that relationship don't see each other for what they objectively are but, rather, view each other in terms of their infantile needs and their infantile conflicts? What would you call that?' And Bak looked over at me ironically and said. 'I'd call that life.' "

2. The point was insightfully made by Emma Goldman: "The tragedy [of educated women] does not lie in too many but in too few experiences." As quoted by John Chalberg in *Emma Goldman* (N.Y.: Harper Collins, 1991), p. 90.

3. In fact, it is of some interest to note that in our society the expression *legally married* is a redundancy, since marriage is essentially a legal institution. But need it be? I don't think so. In fact, from a different perspective, it might be viewed as essentially a religious institution. It would then make as much sense to talk about being "legally married" as it would be to say that someone was "legally baptized," or "legally barmitzvahed." The fact that marriage is such an integral aspect of our legal system reflects how far we are from having truly separated church from state.

4. The following quotation by Sheldon Wolin in Bill Moyers's *A World of Ideas* (N.Y.: Doubleday, 1989), p. 103, seems to reflect a similar concern from someone who has evidently given considerable thought to the issue:

   I think that one of the most important developments in this country in the last thirty years has been the steady erosion of faith in democratic values. I've always drawn a distinction between liberal values and democratic values. Liberal values are values that are basically suspicious of democracy. Liberal values stress the importance of constitutional guarantees, bills of rights, legal procedures, due process, and so on, as protections against democratic legislatures of popular movements. Liberalism has become the home base in which you can agree that you have to have a certain amount of legitimacy to government that can only come from popular elections—but that's the end of a serious commitment to equal rights and sharing. The movement away from democratic values toward liberal values is very pronounced. We talk about it in terms of meritocracy, rewarding those who deserve more because of their skills. But this is ultimately a way of hollowing out the content of democracy. It's not that we're really all democrats today who distrust democracy. I think we distrust it, and that therefore we aren't democrats.

18

Traditionalists and Revisionists: Politically Correct Curricula

I have not read everything written in the debate about politically correct curricula, but I have read enough, most recently Goodman,[1] to convince me that I can disagree substantively with both sides. The most widely discussed case is that of Stanford University, which in 1988 changed the name of its program in Western Culture to "Cultures, Ideas and Values," and decided to include in their required list of readings works by women, minorities, and people of color, hence challenging the legitimacy of the literary canon. The most recent debate centered around the decision by the University of Washington faculty to reject a proposal for a requirement in American Pluralism. It may seem presumptuous to claim that something worthwhile remains to be said, but this seems to me to be one of those issues where the shared assumptions, not discussed, are almost as significant as the disagreements, passionately debated.

Requirements for a Liberal Education: A Contradiction

I take the word *liberal* in such expressions as liberal arts and *liberal education* to be primarily related to its original meaning, i.e., "free, or pertaining to a free person," and only secondarily to mean "general or extensive." In other words, a *liberal education* is presumably a "liberating education." Understood in this way, one may quite legitimately ask how this education, or elements thereof, can be *required*. The answer, I think, is quite clear. One can *require* someone to be "bound"; one cannot *require* someone to be "free." The student movement of the sixties insisted on the distinction between education and certification. In the case of the latter, requirements make very good sense. I think requirements make very little sense in the case of education, which I also take to be related to its etymology, *e* and *ducere*, i.e., "to lead out," as opposed, for example, to induction. These are not merely linguistic niceties, but philosophical issues of some significance.

Both sides of the current debate about the function and nature of the literary canon have tacitly accepted the view of the student as "an empty glass" to be filled with worthwhile ideas and values. And they have rejected what Bertrand Russell,[2] cited by Chomsky,[3] I think quite insightfully, characterized as "the humanistic conception [which] regards a child as a gardener regards a young tree, i.e., as something with a certain intrinsic nature, which will develop into an admirable form, given proper soil and air and light." Or, to speak less metaphorically, virtually all educators share the view that human beings are "perfectible," and by implication, that they are qualified to do the "perfecting," ignoring a tradition in which what characterized humans was that they were self-perfecting, a quite different notion, with radically different educational consequences.

I have participated in numerous, endless faculty meetings about requirements. I have heard arguments for and against, requiring science majors to take a foreign language, requiring Spanish and French literature majors to take a course in Dante, requiring literature majors to take a course in linguistics, requiring phonology and syntax specialists to take a course in semantics, and on and on. I think I have been consistent. If the proposal is to add a requirement, that is to change the requirements from A, B, C, to A, B, C, *and* D, then I have opposed the proposal. If the proposal is to add an option, that is to change the requirements from A, B, C, to A, B, C, *or* D, then I have favored it. I do not intend to appear self-righteous here but merely to suggest that the principle is clear; the more options the better; the more requirements the worse.

It is no mystery that decisions of this kind sometimes have very significant budgetary and personnel implications. Though routinely denied, most faculty members tend to seek allies, either professional or political, and I think it is appropriate to characterize all such decisions as "political," at least in this limited sense. The debate about the literary canon is no different.

The Function of Literary Study

Regardless of whether the study of literature is required or not, there is a logically prior question: why study literature at all? On the one hand, the question is an ancient one, and yet the current debate about the literary canon assumes that the answer is obvious, and that only philistines, or anti-intellectuals, think that there is an issue here. Not only do I think the issues are complex and unresolved, but even more to the point, the debate about whether it is appropriate to include Alice Walker alongside of William Shakespeare can only make sense if one shares certain assumptions of the function of literary study, assumptions that are rarely made explicit.

First, we can, I think, dismiss the view that reading is merely a form of amusement or entertainment, sort of like doing crossword puzzles. We can dismiss that view, not so much because it is mistaken, but because it precludes further discussion. Entertainment, unlike beauty, I might add, is truly in the eyes of the beholder. One should not deny or minimize the significance of "reading for pleasure," but by the same token, one cannot then prescribe what is pleasurable. The justification for including literature in a system of education must lie elsewhere. I repeat that I think one must distinguish the genuinely artistic from the merely amusing or entertaining.

Aesthetics, Epistemology, and Ethics

I often used to ask classes to consider the situation where they were obliged to choose between walking a mile to see a sunset or walking in the opposite direction to see a painting of a sunset (or, in this case, to hear someone read a poem about a sunset). The choice, I maintained, could not be based on aesthetic criteria. I do not know of, nor can I imagine, a theory of aesthetics that encompasses both natural and human phenomena. Conversely, the choice surely cannot be made purely on epistemological grounds. It is patently absurd to ask which will teach us more about sunsets, the poem, the painting, or the sunset itself. I conclude, then, that the issue is, in part, one of ethics. Do we value human phenomena more than natural phenomena, and under what circumstances?

The above is simultaneously sophomoric and pompous, but I do not think we can evaluate the current debate between the traditionalists and the revisionists unless we are more or less clear about why we think that reading literature *matters* in the first place. And there are, primarily, three reasons, not mutually exclusive:[4]

1. Epistemological, i.e., we learn something, not about nature, but about ourselves. I am not sure exactly what to make of Goodman's characterization of the central function of literature: to bridge individual lives, to help us feel less alone. Although he makes literature sound like a surrogate for psychotherapy, a rather different form of self-knowledge, I will assume that we are in fundamental agreement here.

2. Ethical, i.e., we are better people, not in the circular sense offered by most educators, but in the "existential" sense, of living better lives. Stanford University's president, Donald Kennedy, is quoted as claiming that the purpose of broadening the canon was to reflect "the diversity of American culture and values," which has become a vacuous cliché. But if one tries to give some substance to this rhetorical fluff, it presumably means that as a result of such "education," people will behave toward one

another in more compassionate, accepting, affectionate, and, ultimately, more rewarding ways. The trouble with this claim is that it is so easy to falsify: some of the most criminal acts of our times have been engineered by the product of a "liberal education." This aspiration may be noble, but it just promises too much. Reading the classics may not have caused the holocaust or the Vietnam War; but by the same token, it did not prevent them, either. Or, to put it differently, the advertising hucksters who target black teenagers with commercials for alcohol and cigarettes may quite correctly claim to be sensitive to cultural differences, but that does not make their actions any less reprehensible. In other words, the educators' slogan that "knowledge is virtue" is often false. Knowledge becomes virtue when it is transformed into virtuous actions. It should be no surprise to discover that this rationale for the teaching of literature is just one more version of the fundamentalist's argument for reading the Bible, which in turn is merely the reverse side of the puritanical argument against reading pornography. In all three cases, there is a simplistic assumption about the causal connection between words and deeds, the view that "You are what you read."

None of this is meant to imply that we cannot be moved or affected by literature (or the Bible, or pornography), but the impact is largely random and can only be determined after the fact. It is as though we required everyone to be vaccinated, knowing that we could never determine the identity of the small number who were actually helped.

3. Aesthetic, i.e., we have encountered and appreciated something of artistic worth (produced by humans),[5] and that is a source of wonder and gratification, an issue to which I return below.

Objectivity and Subjectivity in Literary Study

Revisionists who have lasted this far will now roll their eyes and dismiss the above as another attempt to endow literary critics with some "method," or at least a capacity to be "objective" in their assessment of literary merit. Not at all. I have read discussions of objectivity and subjectivity as applied to literary judgments, and I find the debate almost incomprehensible.

We are talking here about literary criticism, a field where the question of truth is virtually irrelevant. The word *theory*, as used by scholars in the humanities, has little to do with the homonym used by scientists or philosophers of science and is a remarkable pretension for a discipline where many of the practitioners are almost incoherent when they try to support a claim with relevant evidence and seem incapable of maintaining the distinction between assumptions and conclusions. This is a field where vagueness is a virtue, and the tolerance level for mystification and internal contradictions keeps rising. The debate about objectivity is premature until we demand a minimum of intellectual common sense. I have heard professors of literature boast about their inability to make their checkbooks balance, as though aesthetic sensibilities and the ability to produce logical argument were mutually incompatible. Having bordered on slander, I should backtrack a little. One does not condemn an entire enterprise merely because some of its members are charlatans.

Thus, Goodman, in his criticism of what he prefers to call the canoneers, ridicules Mark Helprin for claiming that "the qualities of merit lie in the objects themselves" and warns us to "be wary of anyone who claims 'objectivity' for himself, particularly, 'in discussions of art.' " Furthermore, he advises us, "We all have assumptions and opinions that inform our understanding of the world."

There are a number of issues to be sorted out here. As Kuhn[6] and others have repeatedly pointed out, the fact that investigators may approach their data with some preconceptions as to what they may find is not some fundamental flaw but a necessity in the discovery and testing of theories of any depth and interest. Objectivity has little to do with the procedures for arriving at insightful analyses, but a great deal to do with determining the validity of those analyses. So Helprin's tacit implication that he approaches the material with no preconceptions is probably false, but Goodman's observation that we "all have assumptions," though axiomatic, is irrelevant. In most intellectual activity of any significance, there are no neutral observations. With no preconceptions, all observations are equally relevant. The revisionists are surely correct in charging that the traditionalists have not made a very good case for their claim about intrinsic merit. But it surely does not follow that the only alternative is to dismiss all discussions of intrinsic merit as a white male conspiracy. So, the revisionists' position is either that (1) the traditionalists confuse opinion with fact when they say Shakespeare has more merit than Walker, when what they should say is they prefer Shakespeare to Walker, or (2) the traditionalists are racist and/or sexist, or (3) both, i.e., they prefer Shakespeare to Walker *because* they are racist and sexist.

Subjectivity and Political Bias

Perhaps I have overstated the revisionists' case, but not by much. Traditionalists are said, correctly, I maintain, to approach the data with assumptions; this makes their analyses "subjective," a conclusion that I do not think follows. (Copernicus may have approached the heavens with some preconceptions; we do not therefore characterize the heliocentric theory of the planets as subjective.[7]) In any case, there is an additional step taken by revisionists; subjectivity now becomes synonymous with a political bias. Traditionalists and revisionists are both said to have a political agenda; the traditionalists differ only in that they deny it, and furthermore, they deem it inappropriate. I think the charge is legitimate, but I do not, like most revisionists, think it is true by definition.

We are not talking science here, but still one can envision a study of aesthetics independent of such questions as race or class or cultural bias.

Aesthetic Universals

The fundamental conflict between the two camps, and my disagreement with both of them, is most clearly seen in the discussion of literary universals. Again, the issue is an ancient one.

I do not think it is completely facetious to characterize the traditionalists' position as transparently circular: certain literary works last because they have intrinsic (universal) merit; and we know they have intrinsic merit because they have lasted. So much for the use of empirical evidence. But what is the revisionists' alternative? It is not all that clear. Goodman cites the following anthropological evidence: "Laura Bohannan, an Oxford graduate student doing field study in West Africa . . . attempts to relate the story of *Hamlet* to the men of the tribe. . . . She soon discovers, though, that the story quickly disintegrates. . . . The tribesmen are utterly perplexed. . . . "

We are presumably supposed to conclude that *Hamlet* does not embody any "aesthetic universals," or perhaps, more generally, that there are no universals at all.

But why go to Africa? Every year, hundreds, maybe thousands, of college freshmen in the Western world, drop out of (or fail) courses in English literature because, quite literally when asked to read *Hamlet*, they are "utterly perplexed." Goodman and Saul Bellow, with his malicious sarcasm about the "Tolstoy of the Zulus," have fallen into the same trap, namely, ascribing some privileged status in the discussion of universals to evidence from some remote and superficially studied society. The danger of ethnocentrism is obvious; the problem is not solved, however, nor avoided, by this by now obligatory reference to anecdotal anthropological evidence.

Although rarely made explicit, there is an underlying assumption that the rejection of universals is somehow "egalitarian" (and conversely, that the traditionalists are uniformly "elitist"). Ultimately, the question of aesthetic universals is a question of fact, not political dogma, and of biological fact at that. That is, either the human brain is so structured that certain (and *only* certain) combinations of words, music, colors, are perceived as aesthetically gratifying and enriching, or the brain is not so structured. Although we are in the realm of speculation here, it is not absurd to suggest that there are biologically determined constraints on our artistic appreciation, and that an investigation into these constraints would result in some aesthetic universals. From the little we know in other areas, linguistic structure being one, such a proposal makes considerable sense. Or, to modify Plato's paradox, "How can one recognize an instance of art without previously knowing what art is?" So, when Goodman tries to discredit Helprin by accusing him of 'speaking in almost Platonic terms,' the attack backfires. Plato's views about innate knowledge of abstract concepts are not pure gibberish, as most revisionists imply.

But why should such a proposal be disturbing to "progressives"? First, because there are people out there, like former secretary of education William Bennett, who actually claim that "we must study the West [because] it is good . . . " Obviously one wants to rebut such jingoism, and the temptation is to juxtapose some form of cultural relativism: differences, with no value judgments intended or tolerated, like the anthropologists who describe societies with cannibalism or slavery with complete ethical neutrality.

The other reason that "progressives" tend to be put off by proposals about universals is that such suggestions threaten their "interventionist" political philosophy. It is usually presented as optimistic to argue that if there are no "universals," then there is no such thing as "human nature," and, therefore, all of society's flaws are correctable. The issues are complex, and worth pursuing, but the nativist's position is usually misrepresented. The fact that it is part of our "nature" not to fly does not imply that we must all walk at the same speed and in the same direction.

And one should not be too generous to the traditionalists. It is, of course, not surprising to learn that the scholars who defend the literary canon are the same ones who opposed affirmative action, though somewhat less vigorously, for obvious reasons. Furthermore, they tend to be militaristic, homophobic, in favor of the death penalty, against the distribution of condoms in schools, and in general (let's not be coy) come down on the wrong side of most social and political issues. The correlation is not perfect, but it's not random, either.

But none of this leads to the conclusion that progressives seem to fear, namely that the discovery of some biologically determined constraints on our aesthetic sensibility would serve the purposes of such an oppressive ideology. On the contrary, one might reasonably propose that such an eventuality would provide the basis for human bonds and solidarity, which would serve to unite rather than to divide us. That the proposal of such universals might reflect the political bias of the community making the proposal is a danger to be overcome, not a condemnation of the entire project, the political consequences of which may, in fact, be rather hopeful.

We have, then, two sides; the fundamentalists, who confuse faith and the strength of their convictions for relevant evidence and logical argument; and the atheists, who one moment argue the proposition that God does not exist and in the next moment argue that God is not a white male, ignoring the fact that by agreeing to debate the second proposition, they have already yielded on the first.[8]

Notes

1. Matthew Goodman, "The Alchemy of Bias," *Z Magazine* (July/August 1991).

2. Bertrand Russell and Dora Russell, *The Prospects of Industrial Civilization* (N.Y. and London: The Century Co., 1923).
3. Noam Chomsky, *Problems of Knowledge and Freedom* (N.Y.: Pantheon, 1971).
4. Of some interest are the attempts by members of the profession to define their goals. For example, the *MLA Newsletter* (Winter 1991, p. 14) reports on the results of a survey of academics on "the educational goals for upper-division literature classes." Respondents were given a total of nine possible responses, three of which correspond roughly to those discussed herein. The others are worth noting, but not because they contribute much to the discussion. The most frequent response (92.8 percent) was to help students understand the literature of the period, a vacuous tautology, which begs the question, and could equally well be applied to comic strips, dirty jokes, or laundry tickets. The last purported goal (11.8 percent) is to help students understand how reading exposes the impossibility of deciding whether meaning communicates a reality outside language. The most charitable interpretation I can give to this datum is that 11.8 percent of the profession do not know the difference between language and music.
5. I take the word *beauty* to be a more or less technical term in some unspecified aesthetic theory, which might also include terms like *aesthetic purpose*, and I assume the domain of such a theory is limited to human phenomena, and perhaps only one type of human phenomenon at a time. Thus, the use of the term *beautiful* in an expression like *beautiful sunset* is the result of an ambiguity that results from a term being used both technically and non-technically. Sunsets do not have an aesthetic purpose.
6. Thomas S. Kuhn, *The Structure of Scientific Revolutions*, 2nd edition (Chicago: 1970).
7. Michael Polyani, in *Personal Knowledge* (Chicago: University of Chicago Press, 1958), provides a particularly lucid account of what is meant by claiming that the Copernican view of the universe is more objective than the Ptolemaic.
8. I cannot resist ending with a line from the Woody Allen movie *Stardust Memories*. After attending a film festival, featuring films made by the main character, an old man comments, "So, from this, he makes a living?"

19

The Humanities, the Law of Supply and Demand, and the Top Twenty

The May-June 1988 issue of *Academe* juxtaposed two articles addressing problems of faculty staffing: Mary A. Burgan"s "The Faculty and the Superstar Syndrome" (pps. 10–14), and the article by Phyllis Franklin, David Laurence, and Robert D. Denham, "When Solutions Become Problems: Taking a Stand on Part-Time Employment" (pps. 15–19). The irony is obvious: high-paid superstars and cheap labor coexist, often—in fact, typically—in the very same department. But there is no contradiction here; the two are merely different sides of the same coin: a capitulation on the part of the humanities to the marketplace mentality that completely dominates today's institutions of higher education. So, if Burgan is correct that the targeting of special monies for special people threatens to emphasize a class system, then so does the exploitative use of part-time and temporary faculty. (I do not have the facts, but I would not be surprised to discover that white males are overrepresented in the first class and women and minorities in the latter. As in the society at large, the academic class system interacts with our racist and sexist biases.) The whole here is greater than the sum of the parts; the two articles taken together constitute a telling indictment of the entire enterprise.

There is one seemingly superficial similarity between the two articles that is worth pointing out. Burgan is a professor of English; the other authors are all associated with English programs for the Modern Language Association. One does not expect to find professors, say, in the Business School anguishing over the deterioration of morale caused by discrepancies in salaries, status, and teaching loads. Indeed, they are merely practicing what they preach. It is in the humanities that the contradictions become obvious; indeed, it is sheer hypocrisy to repeat the noble principles of aesthetic and ethical values on the one hand, and live our daily lives by the law of supply and demand on the other.

Consider, for example, a recent survey, published in the Winter 1991 *MLA Newsletter*. One of the questions asked professors of upper-division literature classes was to indicate their goals in such courses. The most frequent response (92.8 percent) was "helping students to . . . understand literature," which is the kind of vacuous tautology that permeates the humanities. But more to the point, 51.0 percent responded that they wanted students to "understand the enduring ideas and values of Western civilization." The current debate about staffing suggests that this is largely rhetorical fluff; the enduring idea that emerges is that personal ambition and greed are primary and that the noble aspirations about honor and loyalty and integrity are platitudes to be brought out when convenient, but otherwise ignored.

(I cannot resist the opportunity to comment on one other aspect of the survey, which I acknowledge may constitute a digression, although perhaps it doesn't. The last goal cited [11.8 percent] for teaching literature was "helping students to understand how reading exposes the impossibility of deciding whether meaning communicates a reality outside language." The most charitable interpretation I can give this datum is that 11.8 percent of the members of the profession cannot distinguish language from music.)

So, Burgan asks about "the problems in our new prosperity." The answer is that they are the same as the problems we had with the old recession, which, as we know, has been returning. We rarely distributed our limited resources fairly; there is no reason to expect that we will be wiser now. The "community of scholars" was always largely an empty cliché, and today's superstars as well as the part-time teaching associates are merely different symptoms of the same disease. Burgan's elaborate discussion of the "attitudes about education that the public sector seems to have embraced" is largely besides the point, implying as it does that there is some fundamental difference between the attitudes of the public and the attitudes of the educators ourselves. The public is willing to make resources available in order to provide the environment that "big business needs for its managers." But educators are perfectly comfortable with that role and, in fact, have assimilated much of the same mentality. With the return of the recession, we will witness the restructuring of language departments, which inevitably will result in the termination of precisely the part-time associates who are the most vulnerable, by definition.

I once attended a faculty meeting at which the main item of discussion—though, significantly, not on the formal agenda—was the reduction of the teaching load. There were three proposals: (1) reducing the number of meetings per class; (2) reducing the number of courses taught per year; (3) reducing the number of meetings *and then* reducing the number of courses. In the course of the discussion, teaching was referred to as a "burden," and concern for teaching was described as "scholarly suicide." This attitude is neither new nor atypical, but it is nevertheless outrageous. I am not unaware of the gratification that comes from formulating an intellectual question of some interest and then providing a reasonably persuasive, sustained discussion of the issues involved, but there is no reason to believe the repeated lament that productive scholarship is largely determined by the availability of time, nor that it is inversely correlated with a commitment to teaching. People who have contempt for students should not be teachers, just as there should not be doctors who are disgusted by sick people nor lawyers who dislike people in trouble. The problem of higher education, particularly in the humanities, is not the materialistic, insensitive mentality of our adversaries but the self-serving, hypocritical rhetoric of our advocates.

It is axiomatic that there is an inverse correlation in higher education between the amount of teaching and the salary received. It is not hyperbole to suggest that the ideal for academics is to get paid a maximum salary for not teaching at all. And the part-time teaching associate is a visible reminder that the correlation works at both ends. If the highly paid nonteacher is the logical extension at one end, then some version of slavery is the corresponding extreme at the other. It is no accident that our tolerance level seems to be expanding in both directions. It is a measure of our callousness that the common-sense proposal that we hire full-time, tenure-track faculty, instead of continuing the ethically questionable practice of exploiting part-time staff, is characterized by the editor of *Academe* (P.S.) as "difficult but courageous," when it is neither. Why has the obvious become difficult and courageous?

The distinction between the superstar and the part-time teaching associate reflects another fundamental dichotomy in foreign-language departments and, as far as I can tell, in English departments as well, namely, the twin concerns of language and literature. The teaching associate is hired to staff elementary language (or English composition) classes; the superstar not only does not teach language classes but typically has contempt for those who do. Together they reflect a kind of academic colonialism in which elementary language classes provide the statistical rationale for the exercise of personal ambition by the superstars. The language program is marginalized when it is staffed by second-class citizens in an educational climate in which what matters are national rankings, outside offers, economic viability, and visibility rather than substance.

The issues are complex ones, and I do not wish to trivialize them. But any serious discussion of the integration of the language component into a contemporary language department has to confront one obvious fact: children develop tacit linguistic knowledge at ages three and four. Converting that process into an intellectual exercise for adults requires an extraordinary amount of mystification. The contemporary language department typically is dishonest at both ends. On the one hand, it is incapable of acknowledging that a great deal of what they do is intellectually suspect, but on the other hand, it is willing to exploit those of their colleagues who are prepared to take language instruction seriously.

One might wonder why students are so acquiescent in the face of this widespread indifference to teaching on the part of the faculty. It is not as if they are unaware of it. The indifference is common knowledge. But students are co-conspirators here. For a large majority of the students, the best possible news is that today's class has been canceled. I cannot off-hand think of a comparable segment of society where consumers willingly pay for absolutely nothing. Imagine going to a doctor, being told that the doctor is not in, but receiving the same bill. No rain checks, no refunds, rarely even an apology.

I recall a Faculty Senate meeting in the sixties, where the faculty debated the inappropriateness of canceling classes in protest of the killing of students at Kent State and Jackson State. One faculty member, less hypocritical than most, pointed out that we rarely objected to a faculty member's cancelation of classes to attend a professional meeting or even for a dentist appointment. However, the political rationale, he maintained, was unacceptable. In an institution where certification has replaced education, there is a tacit understanding; teachers agree to certify virtually all students as long as students refrain from blowing the whistle on incompetent teachers. Educational malpractice is the norm, and truth in advertising has not yet reached our institutions of higher learning.

Of some interest in this connection is the prevalence of student cheating. Michael Moore, the author of a book on cheating by college students, blames professors and "the system." Students cheat, he maintains (*Seattle Times*, January 17, 1992) "in classes they are forced to take . . . in classes that are boring." But he is too easy on himself. In today's society, cheating constitutes less of a moral dilemma than speeding. Students cheat because they have been persuaded that their transcript is more important than their education. There are anecdotes of medical students cheating to raise their grades on a test from 95 to 97. This has nothing to do with boring requirements but is a consequence of the emphasis on certification and education as

100

a means not an end. I used to encourage students in my classes to work jointly to co-author their required papers. The idea was not very successful. The concept of genuine cooperation for their mutual advantage is alien to most students. In contrast, the frequent advice that professors give promising students about some activity or service "looking good on their resumé" reflects in a particularly indicting way what the priorities actually are. A prestigious "diploma mill" must be able to provide its clientele with an impressive transcript and a good-looking resumé.

Burgan observes that faculty members have absorbed "the analogy between sports and academics"; an English department boasts of "a lineup of home-run hitters." The metaphor is perhaps more revealing than she intends. Football teams compete against each other and are ranked in the top twenty accordingly. In what sense, other than the obvious preoccupation with status, can the English Department at Indiana U. be said to be competing against the one in Ann Arbor or in Seattle? Why does it matter that I used to teach students who come from Spokane and she teaches those who come from Indianapolis? Why is being associated with a "prestigious" department comparable to being a member of a winning team? Is it the quality of the students? A university with no average students is like a hospital with no sick people. Competition and community do not complement each other; they contradict one another. If scholars at different schools were in fact competing against one another, then the joint authorship of a scholarly article by faculty at different universities would be some kind of pathological aberration. Prestige, money, and privilege are measures of our vanity and self-indulgence, not of our contribution to education.

One used to hear the anecdote of the university president who pledged that he would build a university that the football team could be proud of. I suspect that university presidents could not now be so frivolous because the joke has become the reality. The humanities will not really prosper until we find models other than the marketplace and big-time athletics to emulate.

PART IV

GAMBLING

20

Thoroughbred Betting—a Real Sport*

A great deal has been written over the years about race horses and both people who train and race them, and the handicappers who try to determine how they will perform.

A horse race provides a unique combination of a sports event and legalized gambling, and as such has an appeal which is hard to duplicate.

A race horse is an athlete, and a superior race horse is a superior athlete, with physical qualities of stamina, speed and grace, and something less tangible which is quite correctly referred to as courage.

Each race track, no matter how small, has developed a tradition which includes a number of horses that have endeared themselves to racing fans in a way which is quite comparable to the esteem and affection that fans have for a Julius Erving or a Willie Mays.

Add to that, the contribution of the jockey. A famous rider is supposed to have said that "Most people claim that a horse race is 90 percent horse and 10 percent jockey, but they're wrong; it's 100 percent horse."

And an East Coast trainer once claimed that one could "take the top 100 jocks, and there ain't a nose difference between them."

*Originally published in *Northwest Gambler* 2, No. 3 (August 1987): p. 5. Reprinted with permission.

But nobody who has seen a Willie Shoemaker urge a horse to its maximum effort at precisely the right moment could ever belittle the skill of an expert jockey, an athlete who is aggressive without being reckless, in a sport where the combination of judgment and talent results in split-second, high-risk decisions.

Every once in a while, the result is an extraordinary horse race, comparable in its emotion and spectacle to any outstanding sports event. For me, the day Turbulator won a stakes race at Longacres Race Track in a three-horse photo, and broke the world record for 6½ furlongs was such a race—great athletes all performing at their best.

And yet, with all of that, everyone knows that if there were no betting, a race track would be a lonely place. The race track fan is more gambler than spectator.

The dedicated handicapper has a passion which borders on addiction, a passion which cannot be dismissed as motivated merely by materialism and greed, although there's plenty of that, too, at any race track. But ask any handicapper about the special "high" that comes from "a good hit."

Essentially, there are three forms of gambling. The most transparent and least demanding is illustrated by lotteries, numbers, bingo games, slot machines, and to a lesser degree, roulette and other games where chance plays an overriding role.

A second type of gambling is illustrated in playing cards, where no one doubts that there are more or less talented players, but where the opportunity to display one's skill is limited by the cards that are dealt.

But, more importantly, card players are always betting on themselves. The bettors are the players and they themselves determine the outcome of the event.

But betting on a horse race is different. There is a distance between the event and the bettor. There is something "out there" to be understood.

Predicting the outcome of a horse race is in principle no different from predicting any other human or natural phenomenon. Success is determined by the limits of our understanding.

Furthermore, in a world where one constantly speculates

about "the road not taken," here, unlike betting on a football game or gambling in the stock market, the uncertainty is unambiguously resolved in about a minute and ten seconds.

There are a few handicappers who only bet on favorites and do well, and there are a few who never bet on favorites and do well. The former cannot tolerate long streaks without cashing; the latter can.

What they share is a certain self-knowledge and discipline. It's not enough to know something about race horses in order to be a successful handicapper; one has to know one's own weaknesses and limitations as well.

The gamblers who win at the track have learned something about an admittedly narrow segment of the world, but more importantly, they have discovered something about themselves, too.

21

Gambling, Theory Construction, and the Left*

Introduction

As a member of the faculty of a large university and as someone usually associated with progressive causes, I am repeatedly challenged to justify my interest in horse racing and handicapping. The assumptions of friends and colleagues are quite clear: (1) trying to predict the winner of a horse race cannot ultimately be intellectually rewarding, and (2) gambling in general, and betting on the horses in particular, is politically suspect.

Handicapping as Theory Construction

Let me consider the intellectual argument first. The unsophisticated, when pressed for an elaboration on the view that there is no interesting theory construction involved, usually respond with one or both of the following: "It's all luck," or "It's all corrupt," ignoring the fact that the two are mutually incompatible. (It could, I guess, be true that the outcome of a race is determined by *only* luck and corruption, in some unspecified proportion.)

*To be published in *New Left Review*. Used with permission.

Now, there are forms of gambling that are virtually all the result of chance, lotteries, roulette, bingo games, etc., being typical examples. There is nothing "out there" to be understood, and consequently it is not clear what insights the player could be trying to develop, which is why it was so funny to hear a gambling friend suggest that we get together for lunch, "to handicap the lottery." But clearly that does not apply to a horse race. The outcome of a sporting event is not random. What racing fans refer to as "racing luck" includes a range of low-probability phenomena, e.g., getting left at the gate, which merely increases the number of variables and hence complicates any calculations. As a result, even the most talented handicapper expects only partial success, but that is logically quite different from a genuinely random distribution.

Similarly, for "corruption." It is undoubtedly true that some trainers use illegal drugs, jockeys use mechanical devices that are prohibited, and there are attempts at "fixing" races. But in the last analysis, these too are nothing more than confounding variables. Indeed, "corruption" is a variable that the astute handicapper may be able to exploit. As far as I can see, there is no conceptual difficulty here. The ability to predict the outcome of a horse race is constrained primarily by the handicapper's limitations. As in other areas of intellectual inquiry, there are limits to our understanding. Now, the prediction of the outcome of a race is quite independent of the gambling associated with it; but everyone understands that without the gambling, there would be no horse racing. The explanation is not so obvious. After all, there is virtually no gambling on races between humans; nevertheless, track-and-field events develop a considerable following and are even given worldwide significance during the Olympics. The horse race fan is more gambler than spectator, and a horse race without wagering would be like spinning a roulette wheel without betting—of very limited interest.

And it is the gambling that makes the comparison between handicapping and other forms of theory construction so problematic. There is nothing in science analogous to the element of "profitability," which is at the basis of handicapping. Take two gamblers, A and B. Gambler A bets favorites and picks 33 percent winners, with an average payoff of $5.40 for a $2 bet; hence, he/she loses 60 cents for every $6 bet for a net loss of 10 percent. Gambler B bets long shots, picks 10 percent winners with an average payoff of $22.00; thus, he/she wins $2 for every $20 bet for a net gain of 10 percent. There is no ambiguity here; we conclude that B is the superior handicapper. It is as if a scientific community systematically disregarded theories that accounted correctly for large amounts of data in favor of the theory that missed all the obvious facts but predicted the anomalous, hard-to-explain phenomena.

But note also that the superior handicapper, B, also knows something about himself/herself. Such a gambler must have a tolerance for long losing streaks, which gambler A may find incomprehensible and personally unacceptable. And, ultimately, therein lies the appeal of handicapping; it combines the attempt to understand an admittedly limited universe with self-knowledge. Success is the result of the delicate interaction of the two.

Animal Genetics

The distinction between humans and thoroughbreds is of some interest since it provides the basis for an area of inquiry that is accepted as the legitimate province of science with virtually no controversy at all, namely the genetics of horse racing. Animal genetics is an academically respected discipline. Thus, a recent newspaper article (*Washington Post*, May 2, 1988) reports on research by animal geneticists, addressing the "riddle" of why today's race horses aren't faster than those of generations past. "It is a mystery that scientists find especially intriguing because today's human runners are considerably faster than their counterparts of the past. That horses are routinely bred for speed and humans are not adds to the intrigue. . . . William G. Hill, an animal geneticist at the University of Edinburgh, noted, for example, that the time men took to run 1,500 meters in the Olympic games declined by 15 seconds, or 7 percent, between 1936 and 1984. . . . By contrast . . . the winning times of thoroughbreds in the English classic horse races have not fallen substantially during the past 50 years even though the horses have been bred relentlessly for racing. . . . One possible explanation . . . is that thoroughbreds long ago reached the peak of their breed's genetic potential . . . the best horses already carry the most advantageous combinations of genes available within the breed."*

Explanations and Ad Hoc Hypotheses

The above discussion illustrates an issue of some general interest, namely the distinction between explanation and description. Consider, now, the following. The world's record for six furlongs (three-quarters of a mile) is one minute, six and four-fifths seconds. Suppose an expert in equine genetics proposes a hypothesis: No horse will ever run six furlongs in less than a minute. Suppose, further, that, subsequently, a horse does run the six furlongs in 1:01 minutes. The paradoxical consequences are that this confirming instance does not strengthen the hypothesis but, in fact, weakens it.[1] The reason is the completely *ad hoc* nature of the hypothesis. There has been no principled basis for positing 1:00 as a lower limit. So the suggestion above that "thoroughbreds long ago reached the limits of their genetic potential" may be correct, but it does not constitute a bona fide "explanation." What is required is some independent motivation, presumably based on factors such as muscle conformation, lung capacity, strength, stamina, etc., which would yield a specific calculation around, say, 1:05. In the absence of such a principled motivation, the proposed explanation is virtually reduced to a tautology: horses do not run faster because they cannot run faster.

Language and Perception

Some years ago, John Lotz[2] used racing, in this case human racing, to make an observation about language and perception, what is usually referred to as the Whorfian hypothesis. Lotz observed that the significance attached to the "four-minute mile" was nothing more than a consequence of the completely arbitrary use of a given system of measurements. Given, for example, the metric system, "the mile" is not a natural unit, and the "four-minute" barrier would go unnoticed. Roger Bannister, the first runner to run a mile under four minutes, became famous as a result of a cultural/linguistic accident. Lotz observed further that in addition to arithmetic factors ("the numbers involved are simple integers . . . 'round figures,'" e.g., a baseball batting average of .400), there were linguistic factors (the "expressions of the ideal targets readily lend themselves to analysis and interpretation by reason of their morphemic simplicity and semantic-conceptual transparency . . . trying to run 1603 meters in 4 minutes" does not adequately translate "shooting for the 4-minute mile") and cultural factors (such targets "presuppose a general cultural setting of a non-verbal sort . . . high valuation and meticulous recording of top physical performances").

The Politics of Gambling

Which brings us to the political objection. The argument from a segment of the Left against gambling has, as far as I can determine, the following features: (1) In contrast to the view that there might be some intellectual gratification, it is alleged that the main motivation is economic: the race track is capitalism at its worst; people are driven either by need or by greed. A corollary: In a society where fundamental needs are met, gambling would be unattractive, perhaps even pathological. (2) Gambling, like most capitalist enterprises, favors the rich at the expense of the poor. "It takes money to make money." If there are any winners, they are primarily those with considerable money to invest in the first place. (3) Poor people "waste" their money gambling when they should be spending it on necessities: food, medical care, etc. Thus, one of Fidel Castro's first acts after the revolution was to close down the casinos in Havana and to make gambling illegal. (4) Gambling and, in fact, sports in general is one more form of an "opiate of the masses."

Each of the above points requires some elaboration and, I think, rebuttal. I do not claim to have a deep, theoretical analysis of the psyches of gamblers, but I think that anyone with even the most superficial acquaintance of a small number of horse players would have to conclude that most "orthodox" Marxists are less insightful than Nick the Greek, who is usually given credit for the observation that for the gambler, the money "is just a way of keeping score." (This, of course, begs the question. If money is merely a barometer of what is genuinely at stake; then what is it a measure *of*? The answer is anything but obvious. Vanity, ego, pride? Probably, all of the above, and more. But is puzzle solving in science so different?) In the movie, *The Color of Money*, a character says, "Money won is twice as sweet as money earned." This observation is axiomatic for most gamblers and incomprehensible to virtually everyone else. It is probably not accidental that the most persuasive analysis of horse players that I know is fictional.[3]

What is implicit in the criticism of gambling, though typically denied, is a puritanical view of both pleasure on the one hand and work on the other. Gambling has this ambiguous quality; it is not productive work and therefore, it is alleged, should not be a primary source of a person's income. The winner is morally suspect, the word *parasite* being the metaphor of choice. Conversely, the loser must be a victim. Since she/he derives no tangible reward, the money is "wasted." The critic finds incomprehensible the horse player's claim that "the best thing is to have a ticket on the winner; the next best thing is to have a ticket on the loser." The gambler enjoys "action" and is willing to pay for it. (I am not discussing here the addict who *needs* action.) A society where fundamental needs are met would presumably expand the sources of pleasure, not restrict them.

Second, the view that the big bettor has an advantage over the small bettor merely ignores the simple realities of pari-mutuel wagering. Approximately 17 percent of the amount wagered is "taken out" and divided between the government, in the form of taxes, and the owners of the track, as well as the horse owners, trainers, and jockeys in the form of purses. The remaining 83 percent is returned to the winning bettors. The big bettors gamble more; they don't necessarily gamble better. A race track with its turf club, private boxes, and club house is an extremely elitist (and racist and sexist) institution. But betting at the track is pristinely egalitarian.

Furthermore, consider the arrogance of a political movement that has so little faith in the people's ability to articulate their own wishes and sources of gratification. The right to take a "calculated risk" needs no monitoring from the state.

I do not wish to paint with too broad a brush, but the division between the paternalistic, authoritarian left, on the one hand, and the libertarian left, on the other, may be precisely and quite accurately reflected in the conflicting attitude toward gambling, and by extension to other social phenomena, like prostitution, pornography, drugs, nontraditional expressions of sexuality, etc. The fact that the same split occurs on the right complements, but does not contradict, any of the above.

Sports and Politics

In a recent interview, Chomsky[4] observes that sports fans "are using their common sense and intellectual skills, but in an area which has no meaning and probably thrives because it has no meaning, as a displacement from the serious problems which one cannot influence and affect. . . . " There are two elements in the equation. On the one hand, one cannot quarrel with Chomsky's priorities: the outcome of a sporting event is trivial when contrasted with issues of human suffering and injustice. But then what form of entertainment or pleasure "has meaning"? The comparison between sports and political action is unfairly loaded. Sports have to be compared to, say, the arts. Does music have meaning? Or to take the art form that most readily lends itself to a comparison with sports, does dance have meaning? Is a ballet dancer intrinsically more worthy than a basketball player? It is obvious that anything that people feel passionately about may function to dilute their social conscience. I would claim that in our society romantic love serves that function. Others have argued the same for drugs: opium is the opiate of the masses. But what Chomsky means is rather different, namely, that "the same intellectual skill and capacity for understanding and for accumulating evidence and gaining information and thinking through problems could be used . . . in areas that really matter to human life." Sports fans demonstrate the capacity for independent analysis and anti-authoritarianism that could "under different systems of governance" provide the basis for significant participation in important decision making.

There are two clichés about sports that are diametrically opposed: (1) "It's not whether you win or lose, but how you play the game." (2) "Winning is not the most important thing; it's the only thing." We all understand that it is the second axiom that reflects the reality of big-time athletics in our society and that the first sounds antiquarian. But I would invoke here a distinction that Chomsky[5] has insisted on when it comes to science: on the one hand, the methods of "scientific rationality [which] . . . in itself has zero ideological content," and, on the other hand, the "institutional structures in which scientific work is conducted" (130–31). If it is now the case that the expression "healthy competition" has become an oxymoron, then that is an indictment of the institutional structures in which athletics is conducted, not on the enterprise itself. If it is true that there is an important sense in which the outcome of an athletic event does not matter, it does not follow that sports have no meaning. Wasn't there a Roman emperor who claimed that the two things that people needed were "bread and games?"

Notes

1. For examples of many such paradoxes, see Martin Gardner, "Mathematical Games," *Scientific American* (March 1976): pp. 119–23.
2. John Lotz, "On Language and Culture," *IJAL* 21 (1955): pp. 187–89.
3. William Murray in *Tip on a Dead Crab* (N.Y.: Viking Press, 1984). This observation confirms a general point about the relative insightfulness, or lack thereof, of certain academic disciplines, a point made explicitly, for example, by Noam Chomsky (see note 5): "if I am interested in learning about people, I'll read novels rather than psychology" (130).
4. Noam Chomsky, *The Chomsky Reader,* James Peck, editor (N.Y.: Pantheon Books, 1987), p. 33.
5. Noam Chomsky and Marcus G. Raskin in their article, "Exchanges on Reconstructive Knowledge," in Marcus G. Raskin and Herbert J. Bernstein, *New Ways of Knowing* (Totowa, N.J.: Rowman and Littlefield, 1987).

22

A Horseplayer Looks at the Closing of Longacres

September 21, 1992, was getaway day at Longacres Race Track, and the prospects for horse racing in western Washington are bleak. The Boeing Corporation, which announced the purchase of Longacres Race Track after the 1990 meeting, has indicated that it intends to go ahead with its plans to build an office complex on the site. No group has been able to arrange financing for an alternative race track. Indeed, the efforts of the various groups that have expressed such an interest have been laughably inept, matched only by the incompetence of the Racing Commission and the hypocrisy of the local press, who now referred to the Boeing Corporation as a "bully," after years of ignoring the sport, because of its association with gambling.

A couple of days after getaway day 1990, there was a press conference in Seattle, Washington, at which the sale of Longacres Race Track to the Boeing Corporation was announced. The Alhadeff family, Longacres' owners, announced that the track was no longer economically feasible. The Seattle press devoted more space to the sale than they had to the previous 125 days of racing. There were numerous stories about the "loss of jobs" and the "impact on the economy." There were articles about the Alhadeffs, who were generally portrayed as greedy, callous, and unfeeling. Joe Gottstein, the founder of Longacres, was described as a "humanitarian," which is the kind of rhetorical fluff that one expects in obituaries, not in serious reporting. Let's get one thing straight. Humanitarians do not build race tracks, and the people who build race tracks are not humani-

117

tarians; what they are are legalized bookies, a term that I use with affection, incidentally.

There was lip service paid to the effect the closure might have on the mutuel clerks, waitresses, and bartenders, but there was virtually no reference to the fan. The contempt for the horseplayer is widespread and easy to document. When I submitted a short piece to the *Seattle Times* a few years ago, I was told quite directly that the article conflicted with the paper's anti-gambling policy.

Local coverage of horse racing is mediocre at best. (On getaway day 1990, Ron Hansen came up from California and won five races; there was no mention of the fact in the *Times*.) Throughout the meet, what passes for reporting on horse racing is little more than the publicity releases provided by the track, with occasional quotes from winning jockeys and trainers. The coverage in the *Daily Racing Form* is uniformly bland, which will come as no surprise to horseplayers elsewhere. An article in a local paper a few years ago referred to the fans at Hollywood Park as "greaseballs," adding racism to mediocrity. And the amateurish way the track is covered by the press mirrors the arrogance that management typically displayed toward the fans.

It is rare to find a reporter who genuinely considers racehorses to be athletes. Secretariat's winning of the Belmont by thirty-one lengths arguably constitutes the most dominating performance in a championship event ever. It is as if the Chicago Bears had defeated the Washington Redskins by a score of 173–0 or 273–0, instead of the 73–0 that is a record for a championship game. Perhaps one can understand the reluctance of analysts to compare horses with humans, but what is certainly not understandable is the complete disregard most sports writers display toward jockeys, whose talent and courage are unquestioned. It is morbid to compare tragedies, but consider the different coverage provided, for example, to the injuries suffered by football player Mike Utley and jockey Angel Cordero, in both cases, injuries suffered during competition.

Willie Shoemaker, winner of over 8,800 races, must certainly rank as one of the top athletes of all time. I have heard an anecdote, which I have not been able to verify, to the effect that throughout his career Shoemaker never lodged a claim of foul against another rider. Whether true or not, the fact that such a story even circulates at all reveals the awe and admiration fans have for Shoemaker. It's as if Ted Williams had never questioned an umpire's strike call.

In any case, media coverage can hardly be expected to be much different as long as the perception persists that horse racing is little more than a complicated roulette wheel. And, in particular, that the racetrack fan is seen as little more than a degenerate gambler.

Someone should explain to the press what "a million-dollar-a-day handle" means, and where it comes from. It's the horse-player who eats the lousy food, buys the over-priced drinks, as well as the T-shirts and coffee mugs, and key chains.

Everyone understands that without betting there would be no "thoroughbred industry." What distinguishes the racetrack fan from other sports fans is precisely that the former is more gambler than spectator. And precisely because of the gambling, the horseplayer tends to be more cynical, more knowledgeable, and more informed about the sport. So, for example, horseplayers understand that one of the possible uses of legal drugs is to mask *illegal* drugs, that the use of illegal electrical devices is routine, and that although never reported in the press, there are occasional investigations by stewards into a given horse's "sudden reversal of form," the prevailing euphemism for a fixed race, or more precisely, an honest race after a series of races in which the horse was not allowed to run. Every racetrack is populated by gamblers, touts, hustlers, and bookies, all with a little larceny in their hearts, which, paradoxically, makes them a cut above the average citizen when it comes to honesty, decency, and integrity. Horseplayers yell and curse, and they are blatant in their use of racist and sexist epithets. When they lose, which is usually, they have a long list of scapegoats to blame: the jockeys are crooks, the gate crew is incompetent, and the stewards are both.

119

The regular is amused if not downright contemptuous of the laughable attempts to "market" horse racing. Longacres tried buffalo races and horseshoe pitches; then they blamed the lottery and the popularity of the Seattle Seahawks football team for the low attendance. In contrast, they eliminated the Pick-6, because they were convinced that "Eastern syndicates" dominated the large payoffs, revealing their narrow provincialism as well as their indifference to their clientele.

What the horseplayer wants, and what there is no substitute for, is the spectacle—dare I say "thrill"—of seeing competition between talented, equally matched, highly trained athletes, performing at their best—Alydar and Affirmed, for example—and to have a ticket on one or the other. I don't know who said it first: "The best thing is to have a ticket on the winner, and the second best thing is to have a ticket on the loser." That's axiomatic for the racetrack regular and virtually incomprehensible to everyone else.

Outside of where I lived and worked, Longacres Race Track was the place where I spent most of the last thirty years. I won't miss having to see a horse break down and be carted off. And I won't miss the day that the four top choices in the last race were scratched at post time because the veterinarian discovered they were drugged, then learning "unofficially" that one of them had died the next day. And I won't miss the spills that cost jockeys and horses their careers, and their bodies, and their lives.

But I'll miss the special feeling of seeing a race run the way I had handicapped it and then sharing that feeling with two or three good friends who understand that the successful handicappers, not only have learned something about horses, but also about themselves. Ultimately, gambling is not about horses, or cards, or dice, and certainly not about money; it's about people. As philosopher Kenny Rogers put it, "You gotta know when to hold 'em, and you gotta know when to fold 'em." In gambling, the bottom line is not always the bottom line.

PART V

NOAM CHOMSKY:
LANGUAGE AND POLITICS

23

An Interview with Noam Chomsky*

SAPORTA: You have always tried to be scrupulous in distinguishing those areas in linguistics where you think progress can be made from those where you don't think progress can be made: what you might call mysteries, starting with discovery procedures and carrying on.

My sense is that in the last few years, the area that you think is profitable to explore has become a little narrower, and that, paradoxically, other linguists continue to make what might seem like exaggerated claims in precisely those other areas, ranging from animal language to "transformational grammar is dead." Maybe you could respond to both halves of that.

CHOMSKY: Well, my feeling is that in what I've always regarded as the central areas of linguistic theory, there is quite exciting work in progress. I wouldn't want to suggest that nothing is possible in other domains, like sociolinguistics and so on, but it seems to me that currently the really exciting work is right at the core of theoretical linguistics. I think it is now becoming possible, perhaps for the first time, to develop a theory with a certain degree of deductive structure; that is, with fairly abstract principles that serve as unifying principles bringing together a range of general conditions on the structure of grammar that have been investigated in particular cases, in the really

*Transcript of a radio interview with Noam Chomsky conducted by Sol Saporta at the University of Washington on October 13, 1977 and originally published in *Linguistic Analysis* 4, No. 4(1978): pp. 301–19. Reprinted with permission.

quite extraordinary work of the last ten or fifteen years. So my feeling is that it's now possible to explore unifying ideas, somewhat more abstract ideas that can provide a level of explanatory theory dealing with the central questions of the structure and organization of the formal systems of syntax and their relations to some properties of logical form. In that domain I think there are really new and quite dramatic possibilities. For the first time, in the last few years, I think it's been possible to bring empirical conditions to bear on theories of the precise nature of logical form; for example, on alternative theories of how to represent quantificational structures, involving words like "every," and so on. That's really never seemed possible in the past. So in a sense, just talking of my own work, I think it has, you might say, narrowed. There is a very specific range of constructions and properties of grammars that I've been concentrating on for several years. But in my opinion, they do cover what one might call a fairly rich core of processes on which the full structure of languages is perhaps built. And within this core, I think it's now possible to propose principles with a degree of depth for investigation that go well beyond anything I had imagined several years ago. Furthermore, many new properties of these core processes have come to light in the work of the past years.

About the matter of the scope of linguistic work, to which you refer, I find some of what is commonly written rather misleading. It is as pointless to argue about the scope of linguistics as it is about the scope of biology. At a particular moment, some topics repay intensive study in that discovery of significant explanatory principles and understanding of mechanisms seems possible, while other topics do not. Suppose that I am right in my feelings that we are, perhaps, on the verge of important insights into some of the basic principles and structures of grammar. Then intensive investigation of this "narrow" domain does not limit the scope of linguistics, but rather may offer a more solid basis for the investigation of other topics that may now be relatively inaccessible, in the sense that inquiry into them cannot proceed much beyond description and taxonomy.

There is no conflict between those who choose to study inten- sively the "narrow" question of the basic principles of core grammar, and those who hope to be able to gain some under- standing of such questions as, say, the use of language in concrete social situations. The point should be self-evident—and is indeed regarded as virtually self-evident in much of the best work on pragmatics, for example (the work of Asa Kasher and Jerrold Katz, to mention just two).

SAPORTA: Let me characterize two stages: the stage im- mediately post *Syntactic Structures*; and then let's say the last ten years, in contrast. It seems to me correct to characterize the first stage as what Kuhn would call a period of extraordinary science; that is, a challenging of fundamental assumptions, an establishment of a new paradigm. And, by the same token, the subsequent period is what you might want to call a period of normal science, a kind of refining, redefining, puzzle-solving stage. And that in this last period, to a certain extent, there is a danger of linguistics almost falling between two stools. That is, there is this kind of pseudorevolution, the exaggerated claims. But at the same time, there is a sense of the unfulfilled promise of language as a mirror on the mind, the view that somehow genuine and new insights into mental processes would be revealed through careful analysis of linguistic structure. Presumably you don't share that perception.

CHOMSKY: No, I wouldn't think of it that way myself. I don't want to suggest that I represent any majority view; I probably represent a small minority view, and people who are listening should understand that. But my own picture is really quite different. It seems to me that if you take the period of, say, the mid-fifties, there was what one perhaps might call a para- digm conflict, if one wants to use that terminology. New propos- als arose as to how to view the whole project of doing linguistics; that is, new kinds of questions . . . in fact, in a sense, they really weren't new questions. That is, there is a way of interpreting the structuralist work which I think perhaps would have been rejected by many of the structuralist linguists themselves, but which nevertheless, is, in a sense, consistent with what they were doing. There is a way of interpreting it which leads quite directly to the kinds of questions that have been the focus of attention within work in generative grammar in the years since. In fact, I wouldn't be surprised if that's characteristic of what are called paradigm shifts. It's not so much that totally new questions are asked, as that it becomes possible to see the import of questions that had been peripherally approached in a way that was not clear in earlier periods.

Let me be quite concrete about it. Take the matter of discovery procedures which you mentioned. In American linguistics—in fact, also in European structuralism of the thirties, forties, and early fifties—there was very intensive work, as you know, developing procedures that in principle, one hoped could be applied in a mechanical way to a corpus of data so as to produce, finally, a grammar of that corpus. Well, a crucial question arises at that point; it's essentially the question of realism, you might say. That is the question, What is the nature of these procedures? Are they simply a device for bringing organization to chaos? And, is it the case that one set of procedures is as good as any other set? Or, is there a kind of truth claim involved in those procedures? Well, if there is a truth claim, then that means that the system that arises by applying the procedures is claimed to be represented in the mind in some fashion. That is, one claims, at least, that the procedures correspond in some fashion to what the child is doing when he acquires language, and that the result of applying the procedures corresponds in some fashion to the mental representation of the language in his brain. And in fact that conclusion had been drawn. For example, it had been drawn by Charles Hockett in a very perceptive, brief paper that appeared in the late 1940s, where he took a very strong realist position and said, in effect, that the grammar that the linguist constructs is a representation of synaptic connections in the brain and that the procedures of analysis correspond to what the child is doing when he works with the data and develops that grammar. Hockett is quite unusual, I think, in taking that position. It was very uncharacteristic of the mood of the times, though I think that one can see that this position echoes ideas of Sapir and Jakobson and others. Still, the general picture at the time is quite different; it is a position that was perhaps best represented by people like, say, Twaddell or Martin Joos . . . or my own teacher, Zellig Harris, who held that the procedures were a device for bringing some kind of organization to chaotic material, and that there is no claimed truth, certainly no claimed explanation, no claim to correctness of representing some mental reality. In fact, all such ideas were more or less laughed at as being absurdities. You might say that a crucial question that arose at that point in the development of linguistics was whether one was going to take a realistic attitude towards the procedures of analysis and the results of those procedures; that is, whether one was going to allege that they truly describe some empirical reality and therefore are subject to confirmation or refutation with regard to their truth; or are we simply going to say that they give us convenient fictions . . . that they help us collect the data on a smaller piece of paper, or something like that?

Well, it seems to me that there was a certain tension in the field at that point. In fact, I'm sure if you took a roll call, the Linguistic Society would have voted overwhelmingly for the anti-realist position. Nevertheless, implicitly, they were all accepting the realist position. And it's easy to prove that, I think. The way you can prove it is by just looking through the sequence of papers that appeared. Characteristically, what would happen, let's say in the forties, is that someone would suggest a set of procedures for phonemic analysis or morphemic analysis, and someone else would come along and say, look, if you apply these procedures, it gives the following absurd result. So therefore you have to change the procedures. Then the procedures would be changed and someone would find something else wrong with them, and so on.

Well, to try to make sense out of that kind of interchange, one has to take the realist position. That is, if the procedures were just ways of organizing data, then in what sense could it be that they're giving an absurd result? Any way of organizing

127

data is as good as any other. But of course everyone knew intuitively that some results were just absurd. For example, if the procedures of morphemic analysis told you that the word *men* was not broken down into *man* plus plural, then you just knew that those procedures were no good, because it's obviously true that *men* is related to *man* the way *boys* is related to *boy*. That is, it was taken to be a matter of fact. We might say that it is a matter of the way the language is in fact represented in our minds. Given the actual history, I think it's easy to demonstrate that people were implicitly taking the realist position almost universally, Hockett being a rare exception, rejecting that position. Well, if you now bring the issue to the fore, and if you explicitly take the position that was implicit in most of the work of the period, and return to a version of Hockett's question, that is, is the grammar that is produced by the procedures an accurate representation of the mental reality? Does it characterize our knowledge of language? Could one propose that the procedures that were investigated in fact do correspond to the way the child is learning language? Then, I think two conclusions immediately come forth. Conclusion number one is that the grammars that were provided by the procedures do not capture the mental reality. They didn't even account for the most elementary property of language, the fact that it is infinite in scope. Even that wasn't provided for by an explicit procedure. Secondly, the procedures of analysis that were used couldn't, by the remotest stretch of the imagination, be thought to correspond to the procedures of language learning. We don't know much about language learning, but it's perfectly obvious that the child doesn't work out a theory of the detailed phonetics and phonology of his language before he starts learning any words— which is what those procedures would imply. So, if we take the realist position, which in my view is the only rational position to take towards the enterprise, we conclude first that it was far off the mark. At the same time, there is a positive side to that; namely, taking the realist position towards the procedures does put at the center of linguistic research what ought to be its central question (and does so, I think, for the first time). Namely, it raises what you might say is Plato's question: How is it possible that we have the knowledge that we do have? What is the knowledge that we do have and on what basis could we possibly have acquired it? That is the question that is placed at the center of concern once you take the realist attitude towards the procedures of structural linguistics and reject them as factually wrong under this realist interpretation; but it has posed, as far as I know for the first time in the history of the field, what ought to be the central question of the discipline: How do we come to have our knowledge? Well, what you might call the paradigm shift, though I think the term is misleading, simply arises from taking the essentially realist attitude towards the question which was implicit in the work of the previous period, rejecting the results—I think it was effectively shown in the work of a lot of people that the procedures were wrong and the results were wrong, and so on—and then trying to face directly the question that sort of grows out of the ashes.

In my view, the greatest merit of structural linguistics was to have implicitly brought forth, for the first time in the several thousand-year history of the discipline, what ought to be its central question. And much of the work of the past twenty, twenty-five years has been directed to trying to address that question immediately, directly. Well, how has it worked out? This will be a little cavalier, but to put it in a few sentences, it seems to me that it's sort of like this: if you go back to the mid-fifties, a number of proposals were advanced of a very general nature as to what kind of devices might be involved in the structure of language to take account of its crucial and central properties. For example, the property of having unbounded scope, of having rules that operate on structured phrases to allow formulation of sentences and interpretation of sound and meaning over an infinite scope. That's obviously the central property of language, and devices were proposed that might have those properties. Now, those devices were extremely rich. Within the framework of those devices, there were a great many possible languages, an enormous range of possible languages and grammars. It seems to me that one might say that the work of the past, say, twenty years has been directed largely to restricting more and more the devices that are available in principle for the description of language. Now again let me emphasize that this is probably a rather idiosyncratic view: I think most of my colleagues would describe what happened quite differently. But it seems to me, at least, that the productive work in the field—and their has been plenty of it—has systematically led to more and more restrictive theories about the nature of the devices that are used in language, the ways they interact, and the ways in which they operate to characterize sound and meaning and their interrelations. And it seems to me that now (to get back to what I said before) we are in a fairly exciting period in which there are several approaches: I have one, others have other approaches, and probably they'll all turn out to be wrong, and something not yet thought of will turn out to be correct. But at least it's possible to compare and investigate approaches which try to impose a richer deductive structure on the system of devices that are held to be available in principle for the description of language. Now suppose that these approaches, or one of them or several of them partially succeed— you don't expect more than partial success, obviously, in any stage of science, certainly not in this one. But suppose there is some success in developing a theory of devices available for the representation of language, which has some deductive depth and some explanatory scope; that is, which unifies a variety of different kinds of general conditions that have been noticed, and so on. Well, if that is the case, then let's turn back to the question you raised about language as a mirror of mind. It seems to me that that would justify in the strongest possible sense, the strongest sense I can imagine, the claim that linguistic research can reveal the nature of mental processes, because in fact these devices exhibit such processes in their clearest and purest form. What we are talking about is a particular domain of cognitive psychology; namely, that domain which deals with the structure of one particular faculty, the faculty of language. At the moment I know of no other domain of cognitive psychology where one can propose systems of mental representation, or principles operating on mental representations, that even qualitatively compare with the depth and complexity of devices that can now be studied in the case of language. That is exactly why language is, has always been, and remains, in my view at least, such an exciting area for anyone concerned with cognitive psychology. So my feeling would be that the prospects of success, whatever they may be, for work of the kind I've mentioned add richness and substance to the hope that research into linguistic structures and into mechanisms involved in creating and manipulating mental representations of language—that this work will in fact shed direct light on the nature of mental functioning, perhaps in quite a new way.

SAPORTA: Mental functioning beyond the use of language?

CHOMSKY: That I think has always been a hope that one shouldn't have had. There's a question that arises at this point, a crucial one. It is essentially the question of what you might call modularity. To oversharpen it, there are two quite divergent viewpoints about the way the mind works. There is one extreme position which holds that there is a system of general intelligence, some system of principles of problem solving, of induction, of association, or whatever, which is quite general in character and is simply applied in domain after domain. So you apply that system of principles to learning language; you apply it to recognizing your friends, to finding your way around the city, and so on. A quite different view is that the mind is modular, in the sense that it consists of separate, at least partially separate systems, each with its own intrinsic structure, each designed specifically to handle a particular kind of problem, with the whole system interacting in such a way as to create a very intricate complex of highly special structures. Now, on that second view, which I believe to be correct, the mind would be more or less analogous to the body. How do we think of the human body? Well, it is basically a system of organs. One doesn't expect to find principles of functioning which are going to involve the heart as a special case, the spleen as a special case, and so on; there is a level at which they all fall together, namely, the level of cellular biology, but if you really want to study the structure of the body, you will ask how the specific organs function, what their structures are, what their principles are, how their development is genetically determined, how they interact with one another, and so on. The physical body, the human body, is an intricate and delicate system of interacting subsystems, each of which has very special characteristics and special modes of development. Well, the modular approach to the mind takes essentially the same view; it assumes that we are going to find in the brain—which is perhaps the most complicated system we know of in the universe, and may be the most complicated system that exists in it—what we are going to find there is qualitatively like what we find in any other biological system known to us, namely, a high degree of modularity and specific structure, and that in fact there will be an array of cognitive faculties, call them mental organs if you like—one might think of them as analogous to the physical organs—and that each of these cognitive faculties, each of these mental organs, will have its own very specific properties, its specific structural properties, its specific physical representation, specific mode of development. It'll mature along a course that is predetermined. The result of the flowering of all these systems will be mental representations of a high degree of richness and intricacy, but quite different from one another and interacting in ways which are also biologically determined by the basic genetic structure of the system. Well, if something of the latter sort turns out to be correct, which I suspect it will, then we can anticipate that language will simply be, in effect, one mental organ; that is, the human mind, and it is unique in this respect, develops this mental organ, much as birds develop wings. We don't expect to find general principles of development which are going to include wings and hearts and so on, as subcases. Similarly, there's no particular reason to expect that we'll find principles of mental growth and mental structure that include language and identification of personality structure, let's say, as special cases. To get back to your point, I myself at least would not expect that study of language would tell me anything much about the principles that are involved in other complex cognitive

132

achievements of humans, such as the recognition of personality structure, which undoubtedly is also a complex and creative intellectual achievement. But there is not the slightest reason to believe that it involves similar mental representations; principles of mental computation similar to those that appear in the language faculty. So, if something like the modular approach is correct, that is, if in fact the mind is essentially a system of mental organs, much as the body is a system of physical organs, we should certainly not anticipate that even great progress in the study of one system should illuminate some other system. It's not going to.

SAPORTA: Let me try to relate that to what you said about Plato and see if I can maybe juxtapose two notions. If the question is, What do we know and how could we have learned it? Questions like that were asked about concepts other than language. I seem to recall Bertrand Russell someplace saying, "We all know what it is to be just, and furthermore, we know that we ought to be just." The position that you've just taken suggests that perhaps one cannot generalize from language to other kinds of innate notions. In what sense are they related; in what sense do you think they're not?

CHOMSKY: Well, take that question. I don't doubt that we have a natural moral sense, if you like. That is, just as people somehow can construct an extraordinarily rich system of knowledge of language on the basis of rather limited and degenerate experience, similarly, people develop implicit systems of moral evaluation which are more or less uniform from person to person. There are differences, and the differences are interesting, but over quite a substantial range, we tend to make comparable moral judgments, and we do it, it would appear, in quite intricate and delicate ways involving new cases and agreement often about new cases, and so on; and we do this on the basis of a very limited environmental context available to us. The child or the adult doesn't have much information that enables the mature person to construct a moral system that will in fact apply in a rich range of cases, and yet that happens. Well, whenever we see that, whenever we see a very rich, intricate system developing in a more or less uniform way on the basis of rather restricted stimulus conditions, we have to assume that there is a very powerful, very rich, highly structured innate component that is operating in such a way as to create that highly specific system on the basis of the limited data available to it—exactly as we assume in the case of growth of the body. Why does everyone take for granted that we don't learn to grow arms, but rather, are designed to grow arms? Well, the reason is that the environmental conditions of embryological growth are just not rich enough so that one could plausibly maintain that arms are a copy of the environment. Obviously they are not. Similarly, we should conclude that in the case of the development of moral systems, there's a biological endowment which in effect requires us to develop a system of moral judgment and a theory of justice, if you like, that in fact has detailed applicability over an enormous range; and to do it in a way which is comparable to the way in which other people do it, we share a culture and come to do so on the basis of fairly limited experiential conditions. Now the next question to ask is whether this intrinsic, genetically determined system, this biological endowment which leads to the growth of the mental organ of moral evaluation—whether that system has anything to do with the language system. Well, a priori, there is no particular reason to suppose that it does, any more than, say, the study of the basis for the growth of the heart can be expected to tell you anything much about the basis for the growth of the visual system. I don't see any reason why the same should not be true in the case of the moral system and the system of language, if, of course, this modular approach turns out to be more or less correct.

SAPORTA: You're one of the few linguists who's not embarrassed to use the word *science* applied to linguistics. It seems to me that other people prefer to say a discipline or an area. You take the word science seriously in applying it to linguistics, and, at the same time, in some of the things you've just said, you're not very charitable towards studies of variability and variation, where even some geneticists would say that variability and variation is just the different side of the coin to universals. Maybe you could sort of relate those two.

CHOMSKY: Well, first of all, about the matter of science, my own feeling is that linguistics really has yet to undergo something like a Copernican or Galilean revolution, in very crucial respects. Again, this will be overgeneralizing, but it seems to me that one of the most striking features of the Galilean revolution was that, perhaps for the first time, those responsible for that revolution (that is, Kepler, Galileo, the major figures in what we now regard as that scientific revolution) recognized that depth of explanation could compensate for lack of coverage of data. Let me be more concrete. If you go back to the time of Galileo and look at the array of phenomena that had to be accounted for, it seemed prima facie obvious that the Galilean theory, the Copernican theory could not be supported. That is, there were just masses of unexplained, or even apparently refuting data. Galileo plowed his way through this, putting much of the data aside, redefining what was relevant and what was not relevant, formulating questions in such a way that what appeared to be refuting data were no longer so, and in fact, very often just disregarded data that would have refuted the system. This was done not simply with reckless abandon, but out of a recognition that explanatory principles were being discovered that gave insight into at least some of the phenomena. Now, a willingness to move towards explanatory principles that give insight into some of the phenomena at the cost of not being able to handle all of the phenomena: that I think was one of the most striking intellectual achievements of the great scientific revolution.

So, let's return to the matter of the restriction of the domain of investigation. If you take, say, the Aristotelian world view, the range of phenomena taken to fall within a theory of motion was vastly greater than what Galileo could consider. For example, the Aristotelian theory of motion included not only what we call mechanics—that is, things bumping into each other, and so on—but also growth, perception, development, change; all sorts of phenomena fell together within this theory of motion. The

Galilean theory threw out most of those phenomena, and in fact restricted itself to matter in motion. I think that what was dramatic about the development of physics in that period was that within the domain on which it concentrated, explanatory principles were emerging which could integrate and connect, and give kind of a rationale for phenomena that could previously only be described. Now, as a descriptive system, the Ptolemaic system was no worse than the Galilean system, maybe even a bit better, but it lacked depth of explanation. This shift of intellectual attitude from concern for coverage of data to concern for insight and depth of explanation, and the related willingness to deal with highly idealized systems in order to obtain depth of explanation—this shift of point of view has taken place very rarely, I think, in the history of thought. In linguistics I don't think it has taken place, really. Most linguistic work, for better or for worse, is concerned with accumulation of data, organization of data, making sure that any generalization isn't apparently refuted by some half-described phenomenon that someone noticed somewhere. In comparison, a concern for depth of explanation that may serve to integrate and unify and give insight into some range of phenomena at the probable cost of just not being able to say anything about all sorts of other questions for the time being—and maybe even apparently being refuted by them for reasons that are not yet understood—such an attitude is not very highly valued; in fact, it is often regarded with scorn or disbelief. Until a shift in this direction takes place, I think it would be fair to say that linguistics will not have undergone something like the revolution of early modern science. So in this sense I would tend to be quite specific in the use of the word "science" with regard to modern linguistics, or in fact, almost any field outside of a few of the natural sciences. Perhaps it's obvious, but I think that this is a change that ought to take place, and that if it does take place, it'll lead to a much more exciting and important discipline.

As for the matter of variability and universals, we have to be careful to distinguish several issues. There is, in the first place, the matter of variability of languages—that kind of variability is, as you say, the opposite side of the coin of a concern for universals. Secondly, there is the quite separate question of possible genetic variation among individuals with regard to the language faculty itself. For the contemporary study of language, it seems quite reasonable to abstract away from any possible genetic variation. That is, it seems reasonable to assume, as a very good first approximation, that the genotype is invariant across the species as far as the language faculty is concerned, and to proceed from there into the investigation of linguistic universals and variability of languages. At the same time, it would come as no surprise to discover that there is some genetic variation, and if this could be discovered, it might lead to new and possibly revealing ways to study the intrinsic nature of the language faculty. It has occasionally been observed, for example, that unusually late onset of language use seems to run in families, and one might find other aspects of language use or structure that are subject to a degree of variability—a discovery that might be significant for therapy as well as for research into language. Variability of language within a fixed system of universals—an invariant genotype—is quite a different matter. We should, I think, aim to construct a theory of language that incorporates a system of principles with certain parameters, to be fixed by experience, with the property that once the parameters are fixed, the core grammars of the various possible languages can be deduced. There is some current work that begins to show promise of leading towards such a theory, I believe, though I cannot try to discuss it here. Again, these possibilities now coming into view, I believe, offer exciting prospects for research in linguistic theory and universal grammar.

SAPORTA: I recently had a chance to look again at *Problems of Knowledge and Freedom.* I don't mean to be facetious, but it seems to me that there is a considerable discussion there of certain problems of knowledge, and considerable discussion of certain problems of freedom, and very little of the relationship between those two.

CHOMSKY: I think that's an accurate perception. In fact, I tried to be explicit about that and to make clear that, at present at least, there is very little that we can say, so far as I can see, about major problems of human life, such as the problem of how to achieve a just society, or overcome coercive systems and break out of authoritarian patterns—there is very little that we can conclude about these questions from a study of those few little areas where we've gained some insight into human nature. So in this respect, what achievements there may have been in the investigation of the growth of cognitive structures, for example, and of the nature of human nature, these advances don't tell us very much about the questions we would like to have answers to. The most that one can do, I think, is to note some very tenuous and possibly suggestive connections without claiming in the least that they're deductive connections. In fact, they're not; they're at most vague and loose suggestions which perhaps are worth a little bit of thought. To take one case, there's historically a quite interesting connection between approaches to human nature which have stressed its alleged malleability, and certain social attitudes as to what would be a proper organization of society. For example, if the mind is extremely plastic, if we take an extreme empiricist view, if we say there is nothing to human nature apart from the sum of historically given conditions and that at each point in time, human nature is simply the residue of whatever contingent cultural patterns exist, that the mind as it develops is just a reflection of the materials around it; then, if that is the case, there really are no barriers whatsoever as far as I can see, no moral barriers, to manipulation and domination and control. In fact, the moral basis is laid for coercive and authoritarian society. My own view is—I've tried to argue this a number of times—that one of the reasons why these empty organism theories have such appeal in our intellectual tradition is that they do in a sense eliminate the moral barriers to coercion and control and domination. In contrast, if we take the view that was characteristic, say, of Wilhelm von Humboldt, who is, I think, quite important in this connection, that at the essential core of human nature there are certain fundamental needs, such as the need to inquire and to create, to do creative, productive work under conditions of voluntary association in solidarity with others, and so on, if we make such assumptions, then the question, "What would be a just society?" takes a very different form—that is, the answer to that question takes quite a different form. Similarly, if we take the view, say, characteristic of Adam Smith, that essential to human nature is the need to truck and barter, then we'll develop a different image of what a just and proper society would be, namely, an early capitalist society of small traders, or something of that sort. I think this much is clear: Any view that one puts forth as to the direction that social evolution ought to take—social reform or revolution or whatever—any vision that one has as to the nature of a better or utopian society, a society towards which we ought to strive, or (to be more incremental about it) any point of view that one takes towards the next small change in social evolution, is predicated on some kind of assumption about human nature. I think it's crucially important to try to bring those assumptions forth, and to see whether in fact we can find any evidence bearing on them. Well, to tie all this together, in the few areas where we have any insight, for example, the question of human language, I think there's some reason to accept the view that intrinsic to human nature is the desire to create under conditions of freedom and lack of constraint. Now, that's very vague; perhaps in particular areas we can make it more precise. But if some such characteristics are at the core of human nature, then any design of a just and decent society will have to accommodate to them. Now, I wish it were possible, as it obviously is not, to deduce from our understanding of human nature that the next stage in social evolution ought to be such and such. That we can't do; at most we can draw very loose, tenuous connections that may be more or less suggestive to people.

SAPORTA: When you refer to language as creative and stimulus-free, that seems almost a paraphrase for free will.

CHOMSKY: Well, I think the connection is appropriate. If you go back to the Cartesian period, a very explicit connection was drawn between the creativity of language and freedom of the will. In fact, Descartes regarded the free creative use of language as the most striking evidence for the existence of another mind; that is, a mind that could exercise free will and thought and that was not constrained by mechanical principles, and so on. It would be very nice to be able to learn something about the nature and exercise of freedom of the will. That's what I would call a mystery: at the moment, intrinsically beyond the bounds of human inquiry and comprehension. But what we can perhaps do at least is find some of the mechanisms that are involved in it. Whatever constraints we can discover on the way in which the mind functions in particular areas, these will provide a framework within which free exercise of will takes place. It's not going to solve the problems of freedom of the will, but it will, perhaps, present some of the framework and structure within which that freedom is exercised, and it may tell us something about the way the system in which freedom of the will is exercised develops in the organism, and in fact, even about its basis in our biological endowment. I think that's the most that can be hoped, even by a very long-range projection as to what might be discovered through scientific or quasi-scientific study in the coming years.

SAPORTA: You haven't written very much about what your views are in relation, say, to the views of people like Marx. Specifically, the one thing that I recall precisely is that you reject the interpretation of Marx, which claims that human nature is somehow a fiction.

CHOMSKY: Well, I think you can find in Marx very different things. It's not surprising for a person who wrote over a long period and whose ideas changed. If you look at the early manuscripts, which were heavily influenced by French and German romanticism, there is an emphasis on what he calls "species character"; namely, the species character of free, productive activity, out of which he develops his familiar theory of alienation, which in fact echoes very closely ideas that one finds throughout the romantic period, and in particular, which one finds in, say, somebody like Humboldt some years earlier; that Marx is one who is putting forward claims about the unchangeable and essential character of human nature. Maybe those claims are not very specific, but at least that's the thrust of it. On the other hand, one can certainly find, even from a period shortly after this, formulations which suggest that human nature is nothing but a historical product and that the only common properties of human nature are that it's susceptible to change, and can be modified, and so on. I think the Marxist tradition has tended to emphasize the latter Marx, and I think there's textual justification for giving that interpretation, but I think it's a partial interpretation. In fact, I don't think one can really make sense of the Marxist system on that assumption. For example, I don't think it's possible to give a rational account of the concept of alienated labor on that assumption, nor is it possible to produce something like a moral justification for the commitment to some kind of social change, except on the basis of assumptions about human nature and how modifications in the structure of society will be better able to conform to some of the fundamental needs that are part of our essential nature. Now, what Marx would have said about this, I think, one can argue; that's a complicated textual question, but that's the way the issue seems to me to develop.

SAPORTA: Maybe you could say something about social change, then. You've argued, to my mind, persuasively, that within the context of the university, intellectual curiosity is not an absolute value, that the scholar has to be sensitive to the political and social context, specifically on questions of race and IQ. But at the same time, during the war, it seems to me that you were not very enthusiastic about proposals that R.O.T.C. be moved off campus or that weapons research be moved off campus. You argued the Vietnamese peasants didn't care whether it was done on campus or off, or that that was critical. Do you see any contradiction there? Is there a sense in which you can have it both ways?

CHOMSKY: Well, I don't think I convinced many people of this, so maybe there's something wrong with my reasoning, but as I see it, at least, these positions are entirely consistent. That is, it seems to me just elementary (in fact, sort of trivial) that the scholar or the scientist is no more exempt from moral considerations than any other human being. That is, any person in any of his acts has the responsibility to consider the likely, or more or less foreseeable human consequences of what he does, and if those consequences are harmful to people, then he has to stop. That's just a general fact. I don't know how to put it any more simply. It sounds to me like a Sunday school lecture. I think everybody understands that basically. It's an easy Sunday school sermon, but it's sometimes hard to apply in practice; in fact, it's often hard to apply in practice. Let's try to apply it to the case that you mentioned, the question of weapons research on campus. If one's commitment is to the purity of the campus, if that's the highest principle, then, of course, one will say: Take weapons research off campus, because then the campus is more pure. If, on the other hand, one is concerned with the human consequences of what one does, then the question to raise is: What are the human consequences of having weapons research done on campus or off campus? And this issue has often arisen in very concrete terms. Take, say M.I.T., because I know it best. There was extensive weapons research on the M.I.T. campus. There were laboratories at M.I.T. that were involved, for example, in the development of the technology that's used for ballistic missiles, and so on. In fact, a good deal of the missile guidance technology was developed right on the M.I.T. campus and in laboratories run by the university. Or, let's say, take the University of California, which is probably one of the largest nuclear weapons developers in the world. Or take the question of counter-insurgency technology or pacification techniques, and so on. A good deal of this work was done right on campus. A number of questions arise. First, should this work be done at all? Well, there are differences of opinion about that. Let's take some domain where I think it's clear that we can come to an agreement; say, counter-insurgency technology. As far as I can see, it's elementary that that kind of work simply should not be done. Its only consequence is to harm people, to destroy and murder and control. One can argue that, but I'm going to accept it for now. Assuming that the work shouldn't be done, then the concrete and crucial question arises: Shall we get it off campus?

Well, yes or no, depending on how that's going to affect the way it's done. Now, my feeling is that if the work is going to be done, I'd rather have it done on campus. That is, I'd rather have it be visible, have it be the center of protest and activism, rather than moving it somewhere else where it can be done silently, freely— the same people doing it, often, in fact, by just changing the name of the connection—they can be called consultants rather than professors. The campus will be insulated and apparently pure, but the work is done effectively and without constraint. In fact, my proposal, and I meant this quite seriously, was that the universities ought to establish Departments of Death that should be right in the center of the campus, in which all the work in the university which is committed to destruction and murder and oppression should be centralized. They should have an honest name for it. It shouldn't be called Political Science or Electronics or something like that. It should be called Death Technology or Theory of Oppression or something of that sort, in the interests of truth-in-packaging. Then people would know what it is; it would be impossible to hide. In fact, every effort should be made to make it difficult to hide the political and moral character of the work that's done. I would think in those circumstances, it would tend to arouse the strongest possible opposition and the maximal disruptive effect. And if we don't want the work to be done, what we want is disruption: maybe the disruption will be the contempt of one's fellows, or maybe it'll be something else. But if the purpose to be achieved is stopping the work or at least impeding it, then we always have to ask what's the best device for doing that. And it's not at all obvious that the best device is removing it from campus. Now, it's arguable; I don't have a doctrine on the subject. It just seems to me that that's the framework in which the issue should have been raised. It's not the highest principle that the campus should be pure.

SAPORTA: Perhaps we agree that the university, like most of the institutions, survived the sixties pretty well in the sense that the conservative elements which dominated then dominate now. What went wrong? Why wasn't there more of a fundamental effect?

CHOMSKY: Well, first of all, it's very important to bear in mind that the faculty and, quite generally, the adult intellectual community was never affected very much by the movement. There have been studies which tried to correlate attitudes towards the war with level of education, and contrary to what many people believe, the general result that has come out of these studies is that the higher the educational level, the greater was the support for the war. That is, the most opposition to the war from the very early stages was from the least-educated people. Now of course, those results are subject to complex interpretations. That is, it may be that much of the opposition to the war was of the "win or get out" variety. But whatever the interpretation, that general fact is the case. Now, as far as the organized intelligentsia, including the faculty, scientists, technicians, writers, and so on—by and large, those groups were by no means strongly opposed to the war nor seriously involved in any of the activism of the sixties. Quite the contrary: they tended to take what they themselves called a pragmatic attitude toward the war. They raised the question of whether the war was going to succeed, whether it was too costly or something like that. But fundamental questions about its nature were rarely considered. And overwhelmingly, I think it's fair to say that the universities persisted throughout this period, despite the disruption and the confusion and the activism and so on, in service to the state, with very minor modifications. So, not only do the same elements control now that controlled before, but in fact, they controlled all the way through. Well, again, let me just give M.I.T. as an illustration of the radical difference between student and faculty attitudes—which has generally been the case incidentally. Just two years ago, a major question arose on campus about a proposal to turn over a very substantial part of the Nuclear Engineering Department to the government of Iran for the training of nuclear engineers who were going to be sent by the Iranian atomic energy commission. Well, in effect this meant selling something like a third of the Nuclear Engineering Department to the government of Iran: an utterly scandalous act, in my opinion. Anyway, this came up for a referendum among the students and a faculty vote. The referendum among the students was something like four to one against, and the faculty vote was, I think, approximately four to one in favor. Well, the students are the faculty of tomorrow. There's a gap of five or ten years between them. So, one might ask: Why this remarkable shift in attitude over a short period? I think that it's an interesting question. One shouldn't be glib about the answer. Incidentally, I think this is rather characteristic; I suggest this is a characteristic example. It seems to me that what happens, somehow, is that incorporation into the institution has a tremendous effect on determining attitudes towards such matters and the natural—I give my own value judgments, I can't help that—the natural and instinctive commitment to justice and truth and decency that one finds in a mind that hasn't yet been corrupted by its institutional commitments very rapidly attenuates when those institutional commitments take over. And that's what I think we've seen. The student movement was of course ephemeral. Students come and go every few years. There's not going to be any stability or persistence in something like a youth movement. That can't be the case. And since the movement always was quite isolated from sectors of the society that are more permanent, from a social point of view, it was not at all surprising that it would appear to dissipate and lose its impact as soon as the immediate motive for its activism—the Vietnam War, particularly—was more removed from consciousness.

Nevertheless, one should not exaggerate the changes of the past few years. The moral and intellectual climate of the universities is, I think, quite different from what it was in the fifties, before the impact of the civil rights and antiwar movements. The ideological system that reigned virtually unchallenged at that time was at least bruised, if not undermined, and although efforts are being made with some success to restore what we might call the "state religion"—as was predictable and in fact predicted—still the orthodoxy, conformism, and passivity of the earlier period has not been restored, in the universities or elsewhere. And while the universities do not contain islands of activism or independent critical thought to the extent that they did for a brief period in the late sixties, it should be emphasized that such activism and independent thinking has diffused throughout much of the society. I wouldn't be surprised if the number of people engaged actively in what we regarded then as "movement activities" is of about the same order as it was at the height of the more visible and dramatic activism of the late sixties and early seventies. What the long-term impact will be of the activism of that period is very much an open question, it seems to me.

24

Society, the University, and Language: An Interview with Noam Chomsky*

Introduction

The following interview was conducted during Noam Chomsky's visit to Seattle, on January 25–26, 1989. During his stay, Chomsky gave three public lectures, one on linguistics, one on the Middle East, and one on Central America.

Although Chomsky typically speaks to large, enthusiastic audiences, I was unprepared for the celebrity status he was accorded. It was a little disconcerting to note that the atmosphere at the latter two lectures more closely resembled that of a theatre audience than of a political talk, complete with requests for autographs, couples on dates, and post-talk parties.

It was amusing to observe how seriously the persons who introduced Chomsky took their responsibilities. Chomsky gives maybe 100 talks a year, perhaps 3,000 over the last thirty years, and everyone who introduces him feels the obligation to say something original and "significant." I know because I fell into the same trap myself, when I introduced him at a lecture at the Linguistic Institute at the University of Michigan in the sixties. I spent more time preparing the introduction than I have on

*Originally published in *CRITICA* 2 (Fall 1990): pp. 19–42. Reprinted with permission.

papers that I have delivered. Subsequently the director of the institute ridiculed my introduction for being too long. Introductions to Chomsky have become a genre of their own and seem to have acquired a secondary function. They serve more to introduce the introducer to Chomsky than to introduce Chomsky to the audience.

Chomsky has been interviewed frequently, and often what emerges, both in content and style, are qualities that might appear inappropriate in more scholarly writings. He is a decent, witty man, who can occasionally convert his sarcasm into an appealing form of self-ridicule.

Chomsky has referred to two questions that have occupied him over the years. One is what he calls Plato's problem: How is it that human beings are able to know so much? The other is Orwell's problem regarding society: How come people know so little?

Reading Chomsky's characterization of these two areas of inquiry has reminded me of my own childhood versions of these questions. I remember wondering how people ever "learned" to feed themselves, or their infants, when they were hungry, or who the first human was to discover that rest could overcome fatigue. I assumed that all knowledge had to be "taught" and that therefore the initial discovery was an act of genius. I apparently never observed that other species shared such knowledge.

My version of Orwell's questions is reflected in the following reconstructed dialogue with my mother, the general outlines of which I seem to recall quite clearly.

"Where does Dad go every day?"
"He goes to work."
"Why does he have to go to work?"
"In order to get money."
"Why do we need money?"
"In order to get food."
"Where do we get the food?"
"From the grocery."
"Where do they get the food?"

"From the farmer."
"Where does the farmer get the food?"
"From the ground."
"So, why do we need money?"

Anyone familiar with Chomsky understands that he will often reinterpret a question in an unexpected way, especially if he doesn't share the assumptions underlying the questions. So, for example, one might anticipate that an invitation to compare Thomas Jefferson and Benjamin Franklin with Spiro Agnew and Dan Quayle might elicit some harsh criticism of the latter. Instead what results is a critical assessment of Jefferson and the American constitution.

1. Politics in America

SAPORTA: Let's start with the political scene. Mort Sahl used to tell a joke in which he said that 200 years ago, there were 3 million Americans, and we had people like Jefferson and Franklin. Now, we have 250 million Americans, and we have Agnew, or to bring it up to date, Quayle. "So much," he said, "for the theory of evolution." Has mediocrity become an ideological necessity, here? Has there been a change?

CHOMSKY: I don't think that there's been much of a change. Don't forget that we have concocted lots of illusions about the past. If you look at the famous Founding Fathers for what they actually were, it's not a very impressive sight. For one thing, they were extraordinarily corrupt. Probably the corruption in the first administrations beat anything during the Nixon period. In fact, there's an interesting book that came out about that by an American historian, named Nathan Miller. It's called either "The Founding Finaglers" or "The Finagling Fathers,"—I can never remember. But it's a history of corruption in the United States. He wrote it after the Watergate hearings, and his point was to show that this was just mainstream American politics. He started back in the seventeenth century with the pirate ships in New York, and then went on through the revolution, and virtually every one of those guys were crooks. Washington was a land speculator, and John Hancock was a big robber, and Robert Morris, the financier of the revolution, ended up in jail. Jefferson was an aristocrat, an intelligent man. Franklin is a very mixed story—some of the things he came out with were appalling.

And in fact, if you just take a look at the Constitution—by the standards of the time, the Constitution was a progressive document. But suppose that some Third World country would promulgate that document today. We would call it a reversion to Nazism. That's exactly what we'd do. After all it's a constitution that talks about people who were three-fifths human. Can you imagine any Third World country coming out and saying that there are some people who are three-fifths human? And if you own some of them you get more votes. That's the Constitution.

Or take, say, Jefferson; he wrote the Declaration of Independence. Well, you read that every year; it's the kind of thing you read with your eyes glazed over. You don't see what it says. It's like reading prayers. Take a look at what it says sometime. For example, in the bill of indictment against George the Third, there are a whole lot of charges. Well, in one of them, he charges the king with something like having incited against us the merciless Indian savages, whose known way of warfare is murder of women and children, and so on. Now, Thomas Jefferson was writing in the eighteenth century; he knew that it was the European savages whose known way of warfare was to wait until the braves went out into the field, and then go in and murder the women and children. They had to teach the merciless Indian savages that; because they didn't know how to fight European-style, which is one of the reasons why the genocide of the native Americans was able to take place. They were invaded by a gang of barbarians. In fact, it's part of the reason why Europe conquered most of the world. They were bloody barbarians; nobody knew how to fight like they did. And that's what was happening in the colonies. Well, Thomas Jefferson sits there and writes that the king incited the merciless Indian savages

150

against us. Well that's monstrous. It's even more monstrous that we've been reading it for 200 years and nobody notices anything. But, what I'm saying is, that if you go back and look at what the reality was, delete all the fanaticism, it's a very different picture. It's not that there weren't positive things. Obviously, surely, there were; a lot of progressive things, and a lot of horrible things.

The way that this has been distorted is remarkable. Everybody makes fun of North Korea, Kim Il Sung-ism and all this kind of business. Well, the George Washington cult which went on for years made the Kim Il Sung years look rather tame. Washington wasn't a human being. He was noble, a unique person, he stood above all humanity. All of that was probably concocted as part of a way to unify people who had nothing to do with each other, hated each other, so they needed some kind of symbol. That was a central thesis. In fact the radical democratic thrust of the American revolution had to be overcome. It could be argued that it was overcome by the time of Shay's rebellion, the last real gasp of the radical democratic forces. Around 1776, people were taking seriously the idea that ordinary people can run their own affairs. "We're just as good as anybody else." By a decade later they just got rid of it; that's not the way it's going to work. You just want to be servants of someone else. Shay's rebellion was the last attempt to defend the revolution against the counterrevolution, and the counterrevolution was not only the Federalists, but also the anti-Federalists. Basically, the Federalist conception prevailed, and was written into the Constitution. The Constitution is basically a device to insure that the old aristocracy ran the show, and that there wouldn't be popular democracy.

*   *   *

Chomsky's discussion of the Constitution reminds me of results of a poll which appeared in some publication like *USA* or *People* magazine. Something like 40% of those interviewed answered that the Marxist dictum "To each according to his needs; from each according to his ability," appeared in the American Constitution. Clearly, there are a number of possible interpretations. One is that, rightly or wrongly, many Americans perceive the Constitution to be a radical document. My own view is that the supposedly revolutionary proposal which is suggested by the slogan is little more than political common sense.

SAPORTA: Can you separate out ideology from common sense, intelligence? It seems like today's public figures are an embarrassment.

CHOMSKY: It's not very surprising, actually. How do you get to be a public figure? There's sort of a selection process. If you want to be a public figure, for one thing you have to be power-mad, and for another thing you probably have to be a liar. You can't tell people what you think is true. You have to tell them what you think is going to help your position. Also, if you want to be a public figure, you have to serve people in power. After all, objective power is not in the political system. It's somewhere else, always. Except in a totalitarian state, where it happens to be in the political system. That's what a totalitarian state is. But in a society like ours, or like eighteenth-century America, there's been a split between objective power, meaning the power to decide what happens in the society—investment decisions, production, and all that kind of stuff. That's theoretically separate from political power; it's not really separate, because the people who have objective power also take political power. But it means that if you want to gain political power, you have to know how to serve them. There are various ways of doing this.

Now one extreme case is somebody like Ronald Reagan. The only thing he knows is that you're supposed to read the lines that the rich folks write for you. He's been doing it most of his life, and he's been doing it for the last eight years. I don't even blame him. It's like a child. He just knows that you read the lines, and you get rich. That's his politics.

Or you can get somebody like Henry Kissinger, who is a little more sophisticated about it, but does pretty much the same thing. Kissinger back in the late sixties was offering himself to every politician in sight, saying, "Here I am; take me," and trying to see how he could make it. It's very interesting—because of the extraordinary stupidity. Louis (Kampf) and I used to use his academic essays in undergraduate classes. We had to stop. If you start reading him carefully, the kids start rolling in the aisles. You can't imagine that any human being who could tie his shoes could write this stuff. But one of the things he points out is correct. He defines an expert. He asks what's an expert. He says an expert is a person who knows how to articulate the consensus of the people in power. That, after all, is what made him an expert, and that's the way you become a political figure, too. So there is a selection process. And it's a selection process which leads to the expression of certain qualities. People who don't have those qualities don't become political leaders. I think it's true of any system of power and authority. People who gain the top positions in a system of power and authority are a special type of person. The system rewards certain qualities. If we had no constraints against pathological killers, they would be running the place. And you would find political leaders who would be pathological killers, because everyone would be afraid of them. Our system isn't quite like that, but it does reward certain qualities: service to power, lying, corruption, trying to get as much for yourself as you can—a lot of qualities like that.

SAPORTA: So the notion "public servant" is an oxymoron?

CHOMSKY: Who's a public servant? Anybody who tried to be a public servant wouldn't make it in politics for a minute. Why should business pay for him? It doesn't make any sense. I'm not saying that there's nobody . . . occasionally you'll get a guy . . . After all we do have a political system. It's possible for a statistical error to take place. It's possible for a local constituency just to be organized and keep some guy in office who helps them out. But it really is a kind of statistical error. The pressures of the system are so much against it, that if it happens, it's very marginal.

SAPORTA: So you can't envision what you might call a "benevolent capitalism"?

CHOMSKY: Sure, you can. Just like you can envision a

benevolent fascism, or a benevolent king. You can envision a benevolent slave owner. In fact there were plenty of them. A system of power doesn't have to be savage. As long as the authority patterns are established, you can have various ways of ruling. And if you take a look at systems of power which are untrammeled by any participation—slavery is the extreme case—there are all sorts of variations. There are slave owners who just like to torture and rape, and so on. There were other slave owners who took very good care of their slaves. In fact, if you look back at the arguments over slavery, which after all were moral arguments, a lot of the slave owners justified slavery as moral. And they had an argument. It wasn't stupid. They said, "Look. We take care of these guys. You rent them. You don't take care of them." So, yes, you can have benevolent capitalism. In fact, I don't think capitalism is itself a system of terror. As long as the opportunity to increase profit and market share is available, and as long as you don't get groups trying to interfere with it, let's say unions, then there's no particular need for violence.

*　　*　　*

This view of capitalism seems to me to be somewhat different from the orthodox Marxist view, according to which social injustices, such as racism and sexism are consequences of capitalism, and serve to divide the working class. For Chomsky, capitalism could function even more efficiently if we were all truly interchangeable parts.

2. Acting in a Principled Manner: The Case of Free Speech

Sometimes students ask me to speculate about Chomsky's position on certain issues, and I have trouble characterizing his position on a issue like abortion, for example, because I can see him perceiving it as involving conflicting principles. On the other hand, although I don't recall reading anything on the subject, I have no doubt what his position would be on, say, the death penalty.

SAPORTA: You've always insisted on the need to act on a principled basis. And sometimes the inclination to be principled really creates dilemmas. Here's a very specific case. There was a bill in the Washington legislature that said that the death penalty will be prohibited for minors. It's impossible to act in a principled way.

CHOMSKY: The presupposition is unacceptable.

SAPORTA: It's impossible to act in a principled fashion; and yet, the alternative is to be paralyzed.

CHOMSKY: It's a complicated world. You have to deal with reality as it is. You can't pretend you're living on another planet. You're living in situations of conflict. It's very hard to be principled. For one thing, half the time, you don't know what your principles are. You learn your principles through experience. And for another thing, you find they often conflict. Principles aren't like mathematics. They conflict. You have alternative principles, and they just conflict. And you don't know what to do. And then you have to deal with situations like this, where the issues that actually arise are based on presuppositions that you don't accept. That happens all the time. Let's say, you're working against Contra aid. Well, I don't even accept the presuppositions. I don't think we have the right to do something different than kill them with Contras—like, strangle them with blockades. But you're stuck in this world. So you make your decisions in this world, not in some world you wish existed. Now, in this particular bill, my inclination would be to vote for it, and meanwhile, try to educate people, saying what's wrong with the whole question that's being raised. I don't see what else you can do. You can pretend if you like, but that's not helping anybody. If you want to help people, there's no use pretending you're living on a different planet.

This is an issue that arises all the time. Let's say in the universities. For years, issues have arisen about whether we

155

should try to make the universities pure. Keep military spending off campus; put it across the street. I've always been opposed to that. I'd rather have it on campus. I don't see that we help anybody in the world by having the university look pure. It doesn't seem to me that the people who are being murdered in counter-insurgency operations give a damn whether M.I.T. is pure or not pure. What they care about is what's happening. And I think you can have more of an effect on what's happening if you have it right on campus, and you can disrupt it, and if you use it for educational purposes, and so on, even though the university isn't pure. I don't think the purity of the university is an important value, as compared with other values, like saving people's lives. These kinds of questions arise all the time, in your personal life and everywhere else.

SAPORTA: How about, to make a transition, the principle of free speech? Is that one that you can imagine circumstances where you would compromise?

CHOMSKY: I've taken what you might call an extreme position on free speech, although it's interesting that people only concern themselves with the trivial cases which are obvious, and they don't concern themselves with the extreme cases. Let's take a really extreme case, where I'm not really sure I could defend my position. Although it's interesting that nobody has ever challenged me. In the late sixties, right after the Johnson administration, the question came up about hiring, in the universities, a gang of people who were outright war criminals. I mean if we had the Nuremberg trials they would have been hanged, by the principles of Nuremberg. Furthermore, these guys were not writing about the sixteenth century. They were going to do work which was going to be used to destroy and murder, right then. So should we allow them to teach in the universities? Well, I was in favor of it. In fact, at M.I.T., there was a rumor circulating, which it turned out was fake, it was false, but the rumor was circulated that Walt Rostow was being denied a position in the Political Science Department because of his role in the war, which was the role of a war criminal. Knowing that Political Science Department, it was hard to imagine what they could see wrong with Walt Rostow. I mean by their standards, he was kind of benign. But anyhow, the rumor was around. I think it turned out that it was being circulated by his brother, who was trying to get him a job. What actually happened was that the Economics Department didn't want him because they regarded him as technically incompetent. I don't know why the Political Science Department didn't want him. But the rumor was false. But at the time the radical student group that Louis (Kampf) and I were involved with talked about this. And we decided that we would protest it. And in fact, I went to talk to the president, and told him that if in fact Rostow was being denied an appointment on political grounds we were going to mount demonstrations and protests against it on the grounds of academic freedom. And I wrote about it at the time. I wrote an article which is easily available. It's in the *Encyclopedia Britannica, Great Books* of the year, and reprinted in collections of essays, in which I said that we ought to defend academic freedom, and freedom of speech, even in the extreme case, of people whose work is being used to murder and destroy. Well, that's the most extreme position that I've ever taken. And I don't know if it's right. I think it's defensible, probably, but questionable. You could argue about it. It's kind of interesting that no one ever challenges that, even though it is an extreme position. The reason nobody ever challenges it is that virtually nobody believes in freedom of speech. It's all fraud.

SAPORTA: Whenever I raise questions of freedom of speech, my sense is exactly that. People just disagree on where to draw the line.

CHOMSKY: I think people agree on where to draw the line. They say that we should have freedom of speech for views we like. That's where people draw the line. They don't like to admit it, so they sort of cover it up in all sorts of ways. The reason that nobody ever challenges this position is that they like Rostow's views, so they think, obviously he gets freedom of speech. And, therefore, they won't even look at the principle, and the reason is that intellectuals, especially, tend to be completely unprincipled, and again, it's like political leaders. It's not that if you're

157

an intellectual, you're therefore unprincipled. It's that unless you're unprincipled, you're not a respectable intellectual. You're weeded off somewhere. You end up being a garage mechanic.

SAPORTA: I've always thought that there was a linguistic issue here. If language is stimulus-free, it's also response-free. Just because I tell you to shoot, you don't have to shoot. So on purely linguistic grounds, there could be no such thing as incitement to riot, or incitement to commit murder.

CHOMSKY: Well, that gets into a delicate issue. I think the history of freedom of speech is interesting in this respect. Like a lot of values, these are things you just, sort of learn through experience. They're not written down on paper. So take the First Amendment. Theoretically it grants freedom of speech. In practice, it never did. Until the second World War, a matter of 150 years, there was no fundamental guarantee of freedom of speech in the United States. The government had the authority, and often used the authority to repress criticism of people in power. In the first World War, when the United States was under no threat whatsoever, we instituted legal procedures, which, if Nicaragua did it today, we'd atom-bomb them. It's just horrendous, when you look back at the sedition act, the censorship—putting Eugene Debs in jail for ten years in 1919 because he opposed the draft. Even the victories for freedom of speech, if you look at them, are very illuminating. One of the great victories for freedom of speech was supposed to be the Justice Holmes decision, where he enunciated the "clear and present danger" case. You take a look at the decision, that's Schenck vs. the United States.

SAPORTA: Is that the shouting "Fire" case?

CHOMSKY: You can't shout "Fire" in a crowded theatre. But only when there's a clear and present danger can you stop freedom of speech. That's considered a fantastic victory. That's around 1920. You look at what happened. There was this Socialist party leader, named Schenck, who had published a pamphlet in which he called upon people to oppose the draft by legal means; he thought the draft was unconstitutional. So he said, if you're drafted, go to court, and argue this way and that way, and so on, and he was jailed, and Holmes upheld the decision. That's what people forget. He upheld the decision; he approved it. And he said, well, there was a clear and present danger in this case. So that's the great victory for freedom of speech; a man writes a pamphlet in which he says challenge the draft by legal means; you got to stick him in jail, obviously. That's the great victory for freedom of speech. And that's the way it's looked at.

In fact, it wasn't until 1964 that the law of seditious libel was called unconstitutional. Now seditious libel means challenging power. What you say can be true. Truth is no defense against seditious libel. In fact, the traditional doctrine is that truth makes the crime even worse, because then you're really challenging power. Now that doctrine held in the United States until 1964 in *Times vs. Sullivan. The New York Times* was convicted actually—the Supreme Court overturned it—of publishing an ad that showed some Mississippi sheriff as a monster—or some such thing—I forget the exact details—and they were charged with what amounted to seditious libel—criticizing government authority by publishing the ad, and the Supreme Court overturned that. Now, that was the first time in the United States that the principle of seditious libel had been overturned by the courts, and held inconsistent with the First Amendment.

One of the major historians of freedom of speech, a guy named Harry Kalven, wrote a big book about the topic, which is mistitled *The Worthy Tradition*; it's actually a very unworthy tradition, as he shows. He points out, and I think correctly,—this is a sort of standard scholarly history of freedom of speech—that seditious libel is the criterion for a free society. If a society has a principle of seditious libel, that means that it's a crime to criticize authority. Then whatever else is there, you can forget about. So that means that by that standard, in 1964 the United States began to become a free society. Two hundred years after the Declaration of Independence. In 1969, I think it was, the courts finally overturned the clear and present danger doctrine—it's a horrible doctrine—and they changed it to incitement—so by 1969—I forget what case it was, they ruled that only direct incitement to a crime is not acceptable under the First Amendment. And that comes up to your point. Should direct incitement to a crime be constrained? And that's tricky at that point. That gets into the questions of conspiracy, into another area. Is it a crime to conspire to commit a crime? Suppose the two of us are sitting around and planning a bank robbery. Is that a crime? At that point you get into hazy areas. At what point does a crime begin, is the question.

SAPORTA: Attempted bribery.

CHOMSKY: Forget that. Suppose that you and I are sitting here, and we're planning a bank robbery, we get in a car, and we drive over, and we enter the bank. At what point did the crime begin? That's the question. That's hazy. Suppose I turn to the teller, and I say, "Your money or your life." Well that's speech too. Is that a crime? At some point, the speech becomes part of the crime. And exactly where to draw the line is not so simple a matter. But I think speech can be criminal. For example, if I say "Your money or your life," I think that's criminal. Now, maybe, in some future period, there will be a higher set of values, and people will understand that I didn't understand free speech. That's perfectly possible, but my assumption right now would be that if somebody points a gun at me, and says "Your money or your life," that's a crime, even though it's words. And maybe he doesn't have a gun; let's pretend that he doesn't have a gun; or I'm too scared to look. So. There is some point at which speech becomes criminal. I think that's correct. And where that point is is a measure of the degree of where the civilization is. If seditious libel is criminal, you're living in a kind of totalitarian state, no matter what you call it. I agree with Harry Kalven on that.

* * *

I remain unclear about the relation between conspiracy and incitement. Consider two cases: (1) A person says "I'll give you $1000 if you kill my enemy." Such verbal contracts are surely criminal, and not protected by any principles of free speech. (2)

A fan in the stands shouts "Kill the umpire." Subsequently there's a riot, and somebody kills the umpire. I assume that the fan is not guilty of "inciting someone to commit murder." The issue in the case of incitement seems to be whether one person's speech can be part of "another person's crime."

I recall a case where a soldier was being court-martialed for having written "Kill Nixon" on a fence. Ironically, I was consulted as an "expert witness" to provide linguistic evidence that such an act did not necessarily constitute a threat on the president's life. (The case was dropped, and I never got to testify.) In addition to the "free speech" issue, the incident raises quite serious questions about the use of so-called expert testimony, since theoretical linguistics has very little to offer in the way of guidance here.

3. Mediocrity in the Educational System: Vacuous Scholarship and the Limits of Scientific Inquiry

I have always had a love-hate relationship with literary criticism. Before I gravitated to linguistics in graduate school, the two most impressive, provocative of my teachers had been instructors in Spanish literature. My academic association has always included an appointment in a Department of Spanish (or Romance Languages). My closest friends in academe, both as a graduate student and subsequently, have been in the field of literature.[1] And yet, my impression is that literary criticism is a discipline betrayed. Reading, over the years, the publications of colleagues, at times of promotion, etc., has been a painful and discouraging exercise. Very little of it is memorable. Indeed, I often find myself unable to identify the point of the exercise. It does not seem to further my understanding nor enhance my appreciation of the texts under discussion.

I recently attended a talk by a prestigious faculty member. It was virtually incomprehensible. I might be sympathetic to someone who tried to parody academic scholarship in order to expose it. But I suspect that he was serious: the parody has become the reality.

There is a story of an interviewer who asked three baseball umpires how they went about making their calls.

The first umpire said, "I call 'em like I see 'em."

The second umpire said, "I call 'em the way they are."

And the third umpire said, "They ain't nothin' till I call 'em."

Thirty years ago, Chomsky wrote a review criticizing the proposed distinction between "hocus-pocus" linguistics ("I call 'em like I see 'em.") and "God's truth" linguistics ("I call 'em the way they are.") But that debate seems absolutely enlightened when one considers that there is a view prevalent in the humanities that questions of truth and correctness are irrelevant to their discipline. (Interestingly, advocates of such a view tend to cite modern physics to support their "relativist" position.) An absurdity is now taken to be axiomatic.

I try to get Chomsky to talk about his understanding of scholarship in the humanities.

SAPORTA: Let's talk about the university. You've argued that in certain disciplines, scholarship serves the prevailing ideology, and in fact, one shouldn't expect otherwise. But it seems to me that there's a corollary, which is that a great deal of academic scholarship is absolutely vacuous, just empty, almost unintelligible.

CHOMSKY: You don't have to look very far.

SAPORTA: Is that part of the same mystification? Does mediocrity in the university serve an ideological function?

CHOMSKY: I think it serves a kind of a function. In fact, I think that goes all the way down to kindergarten. There is after all a good social purpose in stupidity in the educational system. It works as a selective filter. It rewards obedience. So take people like me, or probably you, certainly me. How did I ultimately get to Harvard? Well, in part because I got good grades earlier along the line. Well, how do you get good grades? Because for years you do every idiotic thing that you are told to do. You know it's

162

stupid, but you do it. Because you're obedient. Now there are people who aren't obedient. They're called behavior problems, or something, and they end up peddling drugs, or criminals, or something like that. In fact, there are always exceptions, but a system of enforced stupidity has a certain social utility, in insuring that only the people who are pretty much obedient, who are willing to follow orders, will make it through. And that's good, because that rewards the values that are required in a disciplined, authoritarian society, where you're supposed to follow orders, not think too much, because that would be disruptive. So this constant talk about why the schools have to be so stupid—like most things that persist, there's usually some social function in it.

I think that in part is true up to the university level. Although, by then, I think there are other factors. It's just easier to be mediocre. What's scholarship? First of all, a lot of scholarship can be done by an intelligent clerk. We pretend that it's all deep, and that sort of thing, but we know better. The typical thing is you go to graduate school, you're assigned some topic, and you become the world's leading expert on eight years in the seventeenth century, or something like that. You read every document that's written about it. You don't understand anything that's important. Because if you start understanding things, you see interesting ideas, and try to follow them up, and try to figure out what they're all about, and whether they're right, and that sort of thing, and it gets all complicated. But as long as you keep it narrow, and you just do what is called scholarship, make sure that the commas are in the right place and you compare this text against that text, and do all the clerical work, and that sort of thing, then you're O.K., then you get a Ph.D., and somebody offers you a job, and you keep doing the same thing for the rest of your life. And if somebody writes an article, your big problem is to see—did they get the comma right on page 13? And if they didn't you go through the roof, and that sort of business. And it's an easy life. It's a very easy life. Being in a university when you don't have to think is a very easy life. You don't have to work very hard. You get a very good salary, people respect you, you

163

can't imagine a softer life. On the other hand, if you have to worry about whether what you say is true, or if it's important, and people challenge it, or you have to think about new ideas, and so on, it gets to be a bother. And, the result is that if you're then in an academic position, you tend to try to get other people around like you. Why bring in somebody who's going to stimulate students?—make them think about things? They'll start asking questions that you can't answer—start reading something new, thinking about whether it's right, so on and so forth. There are these factors that tend to drive towards mediocrity, and in my view, particularly, in the better colleges, which are more important. My own feeling is that many of the elite colleges are very much over-rated in their humanities departments.

You can see it in our field. Take linguistics. Where has linguistics developed, in the modern sense? Only in the periphery. It was new and innovative thirty years ago. Maybe it was right, maybe it was wrong. Whatever it was, it was something sort of new, a new direction. You had to think, work, and so on. It is very striking to see where it developed, and where it didn't develop. There's virtually nothing in the Ivy League schools, only partial exceptions, Penn and Cornell, I guess, which are half Ivy League schools, where it developed for its own reasons. It developed in places like M.I.T. Why M.I.T.? Because there was no Humanities Department. Nobody was around to stop it. There were no vested interests that were going to prevent it from being developed. So it developed in the Electrical Engineering Department. We're still in the Electrical Engineering Department, basically. We're in the Research Laboratory of Electronics, at M.I.T. It developed at U. of Mass., at Amherst, or take the U. of Washington; it's a major university, but it's not a university with big vested interests in the humanities. And so on, all around the periphery, you get little bits and pieces of it. Not at Harvard, not at Yale, Princeton, which made its first appointment, after all these years, and in fact, that was true because of the pressure of the Philosophy Department, which happens to be a bright, exciting department. They've been pushing for it. And what's more this pattern is repeated everywhere around the world. Everywhere where the field developed, you get the same thing happening. You go to France, let's say. It was Vincennes. Linguistics developed in the part of the Sorbonne which was set up out in the suburbs, to drain off annoying Third World Students and radicals. That's where it developed. And it remains the case. The best linguists are around the periphery, not in the main positions. Take Holland; Tilburg, not Amsterdam. Or Japan. It's not in the University of Tokyo. I think it's the same pattern everywhere. And I don't think it's an accident, either. It's quite different in the sciences. The reason is, that in the sciences you have nature out there keeping you honest. You can do crummy work in the sciences, too, but you can't lie, or you can't lie too long. You're just going to get caught up. And if you do stuff that's not important, somebody else is going to do something that is important, and you're going to be out of luck. So there's a lot of hack work in the sciences. But somebody else is going to do interesting work, and nature is there, forcing you to be honest, forcing you to be creative. Now that simply isn't true in the humanities. There just aren't those external constraints. You can do nonsense about history or literature, for as long as you like. It's not going to come up against the rock of reality.

SAPORTA: You said someplace that when you want to find out about people, you don't read what psychologists do, you read a novel. My reaction immediately to that was, where do you go to find out about novels? That's a non-discipline.

CHOMSKY: I like to read people like Edmund Wilson. I learn something from him. I don't know much literary theory. In fact, I know nothing about it. But what happened in the last decade or so, I think is kind of interesting. I should say, that when I read contemporary literary theory, which I try once in a while, I just can't understand—I mean the words—as far as I'm concerned, they could say it backwards, and it would come out the same. Now, there are two possibilities. They tell you that it's terribly profound, that they've made fantastic leaps forward and it's just incredible. Maybe so. I mean, it's possible that I'm just too dumb to understand it. That's possible. But I'm skeptical.

165

Because I have studied things that are supposed to be hard. So when I read a book in contemporary set theory, I also don't understand it. But I know what I have to do to understand it. And I know I can do it, because I've done it in the past. Maybe I can't prove the theorems, but I can figure out what they're talking about. And when I open up a modern book on quantum theory, I don't understand it either, but again, I know I could understand it at some level. And I know exactly the steps I would have to take. When I open a book by Jacques Derrida, I think I could look at that page for the rest of my life and I'd never understand it. Well, maybe it is so much deeper than quantum physics, that I'm just not equipped for that; maybe some new species has developed, which is way beyond physics and mathematics and all this stuff that we thought was hard. That's a logical possibility, but I somehow know these guys, and I don't see it, I'll tell you that. So the other possibility is that it's a fraud. And they're kidding themselves, and kidding each other. I think that's a fair speculation.

SAPORTA: Well, that raises a dilemma for a university. Because on the one hand, you'd like to encourage the broadest range of inquiry, and yet you don't want to tolerate fraud. There should be some kind of a Hippocratic Oath for professors.

CHOMSKY: There should be. But I don't know how to enforce those rules. I think the mechanisms for enforcement would probably make the disease worse than it is. So you live with it. I think the only way to enforce it is to try to inculcate habits of honesty among students. That's the only place where change can come. Not in the faculty; they have vested interests. For one thing they have vested interests in protecting the professional guilds.

My story is very striking. As you know perfectly well, I don't have any professional credentials. I've never taken a basic course in historical linguistics. I know what I've read in Jespersen. I don't know the field, which is another reason why I'm teaching at M.I.T. And my own work is very idiosyncratic; it ranges way over the goddamn place. But, I've had this experience over and over again. When I was working in mathematical linguistics, I scarcely had an undergraduate course in mathematics. I'm almost completely self-educated. And of course, it shows. If I talk to a professional mathematician for three seconds, he knows that he's not talking to a professional mathematician. But when I get invited to give a graduate math colloquium at Harvard, nobody asks me whether I'm qualified. Nobody stands up and says, "Why is this guy allowed to talk? Where's his degree?" On the other hand, when you ask the Middle East Department to sponsor my talk, they refuse, because I don't have the professional credentials. I'm constantly refused the right to talk in the political sciences, in the Middle East centers, and so on, because I don't have the right credentials. Now, how come the mathematicians don't care, and the Middle East specialists worry about it? The answer to that is pretty obvious. The mathematicians don't care because they're not defensive. They don't care whether I have professional credentials. They want to know if it makes any sense, if it's interesting, or can be fixed up, or if they can make it better than it is, or something. The political scientists are afraid that people will understand that anybody on the street can understand it, if they reduce the three syllable words to one syllable. So, therefore, they have to protect it by a guild system. It's like a priestly caste. You can only allow people in when they've learned the proper incantations, because otherwise people will see that it's pretty empty. An awful lot of academic life is like that.

When I got started in this, I did some work on the history of linguistics, back in the sixties, and the people in the field went berserk. I'll mention a story involving one respected scholar. I had given some lectures at Princeton in 1964 on the history of linguistics, which he had heard about. I was in England shortly afterwards, and I met him on the steps of the British Museum. He virtually pleaded with me to stop working in the area. And I understood exactly why. I mean, here's this tiny little discipline, where nobody ever looked at it. You edit some seventeenth-century grammar, and nobody bothers you, and you know more about it than anyone else, and that sort of thing. Suppose somebody comes along, and says, "Hey, this stuff is really interesting, maybe we ought to think about it, and try to figure out what these guys were talking about." Then you're out of luck. Then you got to start thinking, you got to have ideas, you got to understand things. In fact, when I then published something about it, there was a review in *Language* that was just unbelievable. No professional journal in the sciences would sink to that level. It was full of outrageous lies, so bad I never even responded to it. You can't allow a non-professional to say there's something interesting about this field. And in fact, since then, there's been hysteria. In fact, nobody has found anything that's wrong, or anything like that. It's just hysteria. Suppose it was wrong. Why be hysterical about it? Suppose I had misquoted somebody. Suppose I made a mistake in mathematics. Would they get hysterical? "Hey, you made a mistake; fix it and do it this way," or something like that. But when you have to protect a vacuous discipline, the game is different.

SAPORTA: Let's turn the argument upside down. What would a rational inquiry into the study of literature be like? A colleague of mine once said, that it was a shame that Noam Chomsky didn't have an undergraduate major in English, because if he did, then we would be studying sentences like *My love is a rose* instead of *Not all the arrows hit the target*. Why can't we have intelligent discourse about poetry, literature?

CHOMSKY: For one thing, I think your colleague is making a mistake. If I made up the sentence *Colorless green ideas sleep furiously*, someone stands up and says why didn't you use the Andrew Marvell line which says something about "green thoughts?" Would the field be any different if I had said "green thoughts"? instead of "green ideas"? I mean, I could have looked like a professor, said "green thoughts," quoted Andrew Marvell, that's the way you look fancy, but does it make any difference? It makes no difference. The point is this is all sugar-coating, to make yourself look sophisticated. If you want to play the game, if you want to try to win points among the elite, you do that kind of stuff. But if you're trying to make any sense, it doesn't make any difference.

Can you study literature seriously? I think there are people who have intelligent things to say about literature. Edmund Wilson is an example. At least, I learn something from him. I mean, I can read Edmund Wilson, and then go back and read what he wrote about, that maybe I've read before, and I see it differently. O.K., that's literary criticism.

SAPORTA: But that's not a science of literature.

CHOMSKY: I don't see why it has to be a science. What does science do?

SAPORTA: Is there no such thing as a human science? Can't there be one?

CHOMSKY: I mean, there isn't at the moment. Most of the things that you're interested in are beyond the reach of science. Science is a very special sort of thing. In fact, in the modern sense, there wasn't much in the way of science until the seventeenth century. There was careful observation, description, people had ideas, Archimedes had explanations that were by no means stupid, but there was a real breakthrough in the seventeenth century, with the Galilean revolution, you just got a new kind of science. What happened in the seventeenth century, was some new way of looking at things, what we call modern science. It involved abstraction, idealization. It involved really understanding for the first time that the facts and phenomena are of no particular interest. They're only of instrumental interest. There is a rough difference between natural history and modern natural science, in that in natural history, which includes the humanities, it's the phenomena which are of interest; each phenomenon has to be treasured for itself. But in the natural sciences, in the modern sense, the phenomena are of no interest except insofar as they provide understanding. If they lead you to understand hidden structures, and principles, and so on, then the phenomena are of interest. But most of the time they're of no interest. That's a very different attitude, and it led to tremendous successes in a tiny little area.

Most of the questions that were asked by the Greeks are in the same state now as they were then. Now, there's one tiny little area where modern science happened to work. Why? We could speculate, but there's no special reason to believe that it's going to work anywhere else.

SAPORTA: A science of the mind is beyond human capacity?

CHOMSKY: There are bits and pieces of it. Linguistics is one of the very few areas where it has something to do with the mind—even what we can study in language is not the kind of thing most people are interested in. Most people don't give a damn about binding theory. But there are areas you can study, that look reasonable, and that fit the modes of thinking that we somehow are capable of, so we have a science. There are other areas where we can just be interested in the phenomena, and cannot move to very compelling theoretical explanations or discover far-reaching principles.

*   *   *

I think perhaps we talked past each other here. The reference to *My love is a rose* was intended as an inquiry into the possibility of an aesthetic theory, presumably with a set of universal principles and constraints. Although elsewhere, Chomsky has indicated that he might be sympathetic to such a proposal, there is no suggestion of that in his reply.

Chomsky's comments about the "easy life" of academics remind me of painful conversations with colleagues, in which I have always failed to persuade them that the tenured faculty at large universities are, relatively speaking, a privileged segment of society. The complaints about low salaries and long hours are particularly unpalatable when they come from faculty who see themselves as politically "progressive."

4. The Mind/Brain Distinction

SAPORTA: Let me get you to talk a little about the mind/brain distinction, and the fact that it's at best questionable. I remember reading about some experiments that someone had done with rats in which they conditioned the rat to be afraid of the dark, or something, and then, presumably, transferred part of the brain of the rat to another rat, and the new rat was afraid of the dark. Other people tried to do it and couldn't, etc., but he argued that he didn't know exactly what was happening, but maybe some kind of chemical process was developing. That seems very compatible with your view that the brain/mind distinction is spurious.

CHOMSKY: I don't know of any other view. I think it's compatible with the only view we have.

SAPORTA: But then, fear of the dark is in principle no different from a cyst.

CHOMSKY: Depends on what you mean by "in principle." Are arms and legs no different from a cyst? At some level they're no different from a cyst. They grew. But they're very different in the way they grew. It's just like saying is a tree different from a person. At some level, no, they're just cells.

SAPORTA: It sounds like science fiction. If knowledge can be reduced to a chemical formula, then you could take a pill and learn algebra.

CHOMSKY: That's probably false, but it's not impossible in principle. I don't think learning algebra is very different from taking a pill. Algebra, we don't know much about. Take, learning English. I think that's like undergoing puberty. Learning English is very much like going through puberty. Something happens to you.

SAPORTA: But fear of the dark is not like going through puberty.

CHOMSKY: The only reason we don't know—first of all, fear of the dark may be instinctive. Fear of snakes seems to be instinctive, at least for chimpanzees. So it could very well be that fear of the dark is just in our genes, in which case it's not even like growing a cyst. It's like having arms. Not very much is known about this, but that wouldn't be too surprising. In other organisms where you can test, where you can perform experiments, it appears to be the case that rather specific fears are instinctive. So, if in fact they're instinctive . . .

171

SAPORTA: But, then how about fear of blacks? If that's reducible to a chemical formula, then the implications are . . .

CHOMSKY: Suppose I fear blacks. I fear blacks because of something about me. Now, as far as I'm aware, the only things there are about me are physical things, part of the world. I don't think there's some angel up there directing me. So whatever it is about me, is something about my physical being, inside my skin, and that means that it should be possible in principle to find it. I don't know where you'll find it. In my foot, or something. But I think there's something inside my skin that is the basis for fear of blacks, let's say. Now, I don't even understand what alternative there is. I don't understand what we're discussing. What possible alternative could there be?

SAPORTA: How about the fact that our language seems to make a distinction? "Changing my mind" doesn't seem the same as "changing my brain."

CHOMSKY: There we get into a different issue. There we get into an issue which is absolutely not understood, and maybe will never be understood. And that's the matter of choice. When I change my mind, I'm doing something, I'm carrying out an act, undertaking some course of action. If I change my mind, I can only say I've changed my mind, when I could have done something else, meaning the choices were there, and I picked one. I assume there's some physical basis for that, just because there's a physical basis for everything. To say that there's a physical basis is just saying it's happening. I don't think there's any more than that to it. We don't have any notion of physical reality other than whatever there is. That's the only notion of physical reality. So this is happening, so therefore it's physical reality. But what's involved in the choice is completely unknown, and may be beyond comprehension, so that's why changing one's mind looks like a different thing, than growing a finger-nail, or something.

But to suggest that it's not physical makes sense only if you have some concept of what is physical. We don't have any concept of what is physical. Therefore, as far as I can see, all of these discussions—in my view, all of them—the whole of modern philosophy since the seventeenth century insofar as it's dealt

172

with mind/body problems is not really intelligible because it all presupposes that they have some concept of body. If you don't have some concept of body, you can't talk about mind/body problems. Now, Descartes had a concept of body, a sort of intuitive mechanics, things push each other, and that sort of thing, that's physics. Well, Newton showed that you can't deal with terrestrial motion that way, or planetary motion, so therefore, it's just the wrong notion of body. I don't think that fact has sunk in yet. That if there is no notion of body there cannot be any question of what lies beyond body. So all the discussion is not wrong; it's just meaningless. If physicists come along and say the world consists of anti-matter, that's body. I don't know what the hell they're talking about. Whatever it is, that's body. If they say it's strings vibrating in ten-dimensional space, and everything else is illusion, O.K., then that's body. But the point is that we can't say in advance that you're going beyond body, or you're going beyond physics. Physics is just what there is. Period. And one of the things there seems to be is people making up their minds. So O.K., that's part of physics, a part of physics we can't comprehend, but we can't comprehend most of physics, just tiny, little things. They tell me, when I read *Scientific American,*—I have a big understanding of this stuff—most of what's in the universe is anti-matter, and stuff of that kind. We haven't the foggiest idea of what it is. So even just at the most elementary level, the understanding is like a laser that sort of goes through big, dark clouds, and it gives you little points of light here and there.

*   *   *

Because fear of the dark may, in fact, be instinctive, it may not have been a very good example. But it still sounds outrageous to suggest, for example, that we could put a chemical solution in the water supply, and make pacifists out of everybody. Nevertheless, it may end up being the case that when we say that there's a certain 'chemistry' between two people, we may be speaking a little less metaphorically than we think.

173

5. The Cognitive Revolution

SAPORTA: It's very fashionable to talk about a revolution in views of psychology and cognitive disciplines. My impression is that a lot of that is just lip service, that people still have maintained a hard core of empiricism that's immutable, almost. People will say, "Society reinforces you to believe such-and-such," or "You're conditioned to believe . . ." as if values and beliefs are determined by reinforcement and conditioning. Now, obviously, one doesn't condemn a discipline because of the way the terms are popularly used, but it seems to me that here, there's hardly any gap between the discipline and the common usage.

CHOMSKY: I don't blame people for saying that. The main reason is that I do it myself. We were talking before about how the structures of authority lead to the selection of a certain type of individual. I could have said exactly the same thing by saying "rewards certain abilities and punishes others, and that leads to the selection of certain kinds of people." That's a very crude model; the reason I would use it is that I don't think there's any better understanding. So I would use the crudest model there is. It's probably wrong. It's wrong where we do understand anything, so it's probably wrong here. But that's the best grasp we have of this situation. I don't pretend that that's anything like science or anything; it's just a way of talking. It's at the level of talking about the sun rising. That's the best we can do. It's not false. In most areas of human life, that's the best we can do. I don't have any complaint about talking about reward and punishment, as long as people don't believe that they're saying anything profound. If it's just ordinary talk . . .

I think you're right though. First of all, to talk about the revolution is kind of inflated. I don't think much has happened in these areas in the mid- and late-nineteenth century, and the twentieth century that wasn't pretty much outlined at least in the seventeenth century. We can do it better, and so on and so forth, but the ideas are about the same. There's been nothing like a big revolution. It's all pre-Galilean, in my view. So even the parts where there are some really new things, and there are undoubtedly some, they're not radically different. Here I think people like my friend Tom Kuhn have had a somewhat unfortunate effect. I don't think that there are many scientific revolutions, maybe two, or something like that, in all of human history, and the rest of it is little changes. And as people in the social sciences and the humanities picked up this Kuhnian business, as usual, they turned it to absurdity. I remember once reading a paper by a linguist which was about scientific revolutions in linguistics, and it turned out that there was one about every six months. I've yet to see one. Maybe Panini, or something.

*   *   *

Chomsky is more charitable here than I am. Most non-specialists could presumably be made to acknowledge that to say that "the sun rises" is nothing more than a way of talking, and not very good astronomy. But the same people, and many "specialists" as well, I think, would insist that to say, for example, "TV conditions us to associate sex and violence" is substantially more than a way of talking, and not necessarily bad psychology.

On the other hand, Chomsky clearly prefers to use the word 'revolution' in a rather strict sense. However we choose to characterize the debate between structuralists and generative grammarians in the late fifties, the differences were absolutely fundamental, and the fact that relatively few linguists made the switch reflects the radical difference in the underlying assumptions, assumptions which were, indeed, incompatible.

6. Explanation in Linguistics

SAPORTA: Here, I may have misread, or misunderstood, or just disagree, it seems to me that the notion *explanation* in linguistics has changed in the last thirty years.

CHOMSKY: When you say "the last thirty years," what do you mean?

SAPORTA: I mean specifically, from *Syntactic Structures*. In *Syntactic Structures* in the chapter on explanatory adequacy, a phenomenon is said to be explained if it is predicted by some principle which is independently motivated. Now, something is said to be explained if it can be attributed to Universal Grammar. That seems to me to be a rather radical shift, in the sense that what is a description at the level of biology now becomes an explanation at the level of linguistics. It's as though someone asked, "Why do robins fly?" and you said, "Well, robins are birds, and birds have this biological endowment which enables them to grow wings." That doesn't sound like an explanation.

CHOMSKY: No, but it would be an explanation if you could say what the biological endowment was. If you just say that this anaphoric connection holds because of Universal Grammar, that's not an explanation. But if you say this anaphoric connection holds because of condition A of the binding theory, and condition A of the binding theory says such-and-such, and that's part of Universal Grammar, that is an explanation. That's not like saying that a robin grows wings because it's a bird; it's saying a robin grows wings because here's what's happening in the chromosomes.

SAPORTA: But it's still a description at the level of biology.

CHOMSKY: Yeah; that's perfectly true. That's always the case. I mean, what's an explanation at one level of inquiry is something to be explained at another level of inquiry. That's always the case.

Incidentally, I don't really see the change that you describe. Explaining something in terms of principles and explaining them in terms of Universal Grammar; I think the difference is terminological. "Universal Grammar" just came later to be used as the name for the set of principles.

There is actually one change, but it's a little different from what you suggest. What I did in *Syntactic Structures* was—I assumed—that the best you could do there was establish criteria for selecting among alternative theories. And within a decade or two, I think, it became clear that you could do better than that. You could get an actual set of principles—you could really move to something like a discovery procedure. It's a very different kind of discovery procedure. Take principles and parameters type stuff. If that's right, you really have a discovery procedure. I mean, a practical discovery procedure. If language acquisition really comes down to fixing the values of parameters for functional elements on the basis of short sentences, you have a discovery procedure—and a practical one, which is something I didn't think was possible in the 1950s. And in that sense, it's not so much the concept of explanation that has changed, at least for me, it's the feeling that what you can achieve has changed. I think you can achieve a lot more than I thought you could achieve then. Partly because then, we were saddled with the wrong notions.

SAPORTA: I guess I'm sort of bogged down in explanation as being qualitatively different from description, rather than just a broader, more general description.

CHOMSKY: In *Syntactic Structures* and in later works of mine, there's sort of a technical notion of description and explanation, which is different from the one you're using, and that has to do with descriptive and explanatory adequacy. Look at the LAD model. Let's say a theory is descriptively adequate if it's true of the output of the system, and let's say that a system is explanatorily adequate if it's true of the box. Now, both of those are descriptions. But one of them in a certain sense is explanatory. Actually, they're both explanatory, and they're both descriptive, but at different levels. But nevertheless, I think the terminology made sense. Remember that context. You can have observational adequacy, which is totally boring. But to get beyond that, you want to at least do something. Well, at least what you want to do is describe the output—state what the output is. Well, when you've stated the output of the LAD system, you have given an explanation. Suppose you could write a more extensive version of Panini's grammar of English, you would have explained why this sentence means so-and-so, at some level. But what I called explanatory adequacy required a

177

deeper explanation, namely asking why English grammar looks like that. And that's the inside of the system. But, then you can go on and ask for deeper explanation. Why is the inside of the system like that? And then, you'll say something about the genes. And then you'll ask why do the genes look like that.

SAPORTA: So ultimate explanation is . . .

CHOMSKY: Science is always in the process of going deeper and deeper. And wherever you learn something, you ask why. Everything you answer, leads to the next question, and that'll always be true, as long as the field . . .

SAPORTA: What was clear to me, for example, was Morris Halle's example of how you explain constraints on the form of morphemes, by invoking a criterion which is absolutely independent, which has nothing to do with morpheme-structure rules—the simplicity criterion.

CHOMSKY: Counting the features.

SAPORTA: Right. And that seems to me to be different from Universal Grammar.

CHOMSKY: Actually that was the proposal I made in my work on Hebrew. There, I didn't think you could go as far as I now think. So, I was talking about evaluation procedures in the sense of selecting one alternative, but the alternative selected was in terms of a metric, which involved—any metric that we can use is an operation on a theory which assigns it a number, because the only things we know how to compare are numbers. So if you want to have a mechanical procedure, an algorithm, for evaluating two theories in the same notation, what you have to do is have a way of assigning numbers to them. The way of assigning a number to them was to use certain notations, brackets and braces, and so on, and once you've transformed the system through those notations, to count symbols. Morris's example was a special case of that. That's a kind of explanation.

SAPORTA: And to you no different from current use of the word 'explanation'?

CHOMSKY: The difference is that that was wrong. In fact, I don't think it was completely wrong. It was just not very interesting. It was based on the assumption that languages are rule systems. Early transformational grammar was very traditional. And that's why traditional grammarians accepted it right off, and the structuralists couldn't. Because it was very traditional. It was sort of formalizing traditional, intuitive ideas; it sort of skipped by structural linguistics and went back to traditional ideas. And the tradition that went back to Panini is that language was a rule system, and that really wasn't challenged seriously until the sixties, when it began to become clear that it wasn't a rule system, and by around 1980 roughly, it became very clear that language was not a rule system and that means that all the measures and everything based on the assumption that it was a rule system were not necessarily wrong, but at most very peripheral, because what seems to be happening is completely different. If there has been anything which deserves to be called a revolution, which I doubt, it was around 1980. Everything before then was formalizing old intuitions, opening up new data, and so forth.

7. The Autistic Savant

SAPORTA: What you say about language not being a system of rules triggers something else, which I'm at a loss to formulate very well. It has do with the savant phenomenon—as I understand, for example, these twins that Oliver Sachs describes. They play a game with prime numbers. And if I understand what they do, it's absolutely incomprehensible. It can't be stored, and it can't be calculated. What possible alternative . . .?

CHOMSKY: There are algorithms for prime numbers.

SAPORTA: Oh, I assumed there weren't.

CHOMSKY: The only thing about the algorithms for prime numbers is that they just take too long to carry out. It's not that they're not there. After all, take some huge number, and there's a mechanical procedure to ask whether any smaller number divides into it. But they must be doing it some other way. And that's the mystery. How the hell are they doing it? But, after all, that's the problem with everything. How do I walk across the room? You don't have to go to complicated things like how do you play chess, or how do you write a novel. The kind of thing that people are asking about all the time is besides the point. How do you write poetry? God knows. How do you write the next sentence? How do you ask what the weather is like? Nobody knows that either. We haven't the foggiest idea of how you do the simplest things. How do you tie your shoes?

SAPORTA: But when you talk about mental representations, then we have some idea of what the form of that representation might be. In the case of the prime numbers, we don't have any idea.

CHOMSKY: In the case of prime numbers, we have a complete theoretical understanding, actually complete. And we can construct abstract algorithms which will do it perfectly. We just know that that's not what people are doing. It's like chess; take chess. Chess is theoretically a trivial game; it's a finite game. You could list all the games, there's a finite number of them; you can list them all. If you had a computer a hundred times the size of the universe, you could stick all the games in, and if it worked with the speed of electrons, it could simply select the game it wants to win each time. It would be like tic tac toe. Chess is not different from tic tac toe, theoretically. There's a winning procedure. The only difference is scale. Tic tac toe you can write it out in three lines. Chess it takes maybe the size of the universe. But they're perfectly understood, and they're trivial games. That's one of the reasons I've never seen the point of studying chess. Because we know for certain that a computer program can be written, in principle at least, to beat grand masters. There might be some interest if the programs were based on the kinds of thinking that grand masters employ, but they're not. The best programs are apparently rather "dumb." They exploit advantages of speed and storage, not understanding and insight, whatever they are.

Now, on the other hand, language we don't understand theoretically. We do not have a theoretical understanding of language that we have of prime numbers and chess, which are

180

trivial systems. Language is not a trivial system. As far as we understand it, it's not. So we only have glimmerings of an understanding of language, not a full theoretical understanding. And therefore, it's not at all surprising that we can't do things that you also can't do with trivial systems. Mathematics is the study of very simple systems. As soon as things become the least bit complicated, they're beyond the capacity of studying them. Remember this book of George Gamow, called *One, two, three . . . infinity*. He was expressing something that every mathematician knows. The only numbers there are are 1,2,3 and infinity. Fifteen isn't a number. If anything has fifteen parts to it, forget it. We're not going to understand it. If it's infinite, then you can understand it, because you can abstract away from all the complexity, but anything in the real world which is of some finite size, is typically hopeless. You can never fully understand it in any principled way. You still can't solve the three-body problem. How do three bodies interact according to Newton's laws? Nobody knows. Because 3 is too big a number. If you asked how an infinite number of bodies interact, you can probably solve it, because then you abstract away from all the complexity.

SAPORTA: So you see the twins as in principle no different from any other human . . . ?

CHOMSKY: "In principle" is funny. We don't know. It's like the question you asked before: Is growing a cyst in principle like growing arms? There's no answer to that. It depends on where you draw the line as to what counts as principle. At some level, the principle is the same. It involves molecules. At some other level, it's radically different, undoubtedly. Growing a cyst isn't in the genes; growing arms is. There's no answer to the question, are they different in principle? It depends where you are, in thinking about principles.

*   *   *

I met a student that I grew very fond of. I liked him personally, professionally and politically. He subsequently asked me to write a letter of recommendation for him in connection with a grant he was applying for. He was proposing a study on Portuguese clitics. A couple of days later I had the following dream. In the dream, the student, Juan, was building a table, and I said to him, "Juan, the world needs a good carpenter more than it needs another study on Romance clitics." And then we looked at each other, and both of us started to cry.

I have found the comparison useful. A poor table, is still functional; people can use it to eat, etc. But a poor article is empty; it's not the tragedy that a poor brain operation is, but it is vacuous.

I have always had mixed feelings about my academic "scholarship." Most of it has been either transparently derivative, or just plain mistaken. (I don't consider my case atypical.) But I still have trouble understanding the attitude of most academics towards their work. On the one hand, I observe colleagues who do linguistics the way others do crossword puzzles (or, the way I handicap the horses). If I sometimes mention to them that linguistics might bear on general questions of 'human nature,' they start looking off into space; they almost literally don't know what I'm talking about. On the other hand, talking to Chomsky about linguistics, I invariably get the exact opposite feeling: this guy really thinks that this stuff matters.

8. Semantics

SAPORTA: One often reads that Noam Chomsky is not interested in semantics, which is a bizarre reading of Noam Chomsky. Maybe you could say something about what conceptual semantics is like, or what you understand the thrust of semantics to be. My impression is that what is usually called formal semantics is some kind of syntax, and that you're one of the few people that are interested in semantics.

CHOMSKY: I agree. What most people call semantics, like model-theoretic semantics, is syntax. We just have to decide what terms we're going to use. I think the right way to use the word 'syntax' is for the study of mental representations, and the right way to use the word 'semantics' is for the relation between systems of mental representations and some external reality. Virtually nobody studies the latter.

SAPORTA: That's a very traditional view.

CHOMSKY: Yeah, that's a traditional view. Well, now, who studies the relation between mental representations and external reality? Almost nobody I know. All the stuff that's called semantics is just studies of mental representations.

SAPORTA: How would your view of semantics deal with very classical questions of synonymy and paraphrase?

CHOMSKY: In the case of synonymy, in my view, the modern philosophical tradition is completely off base. The assumption is, and I grew up with this assumption, too; I can't imagine how I believed it all those years, but the assumption is that Van Quine, back in the late forties, showed that there is a real problem with analyticity; there aren't any synonymous sentences, and so on and so forth. If you look back and think—all the evidence is to the contrary. What Quine showed is that it's hard to get a criterion for synonymy, but it's hard to get a criterion for anything. That's not interesting. Let's take a real case. *I persuaded John to go to college; therefore, John decided to go to college.* vs. *I persuaded John to go to college; therefore I decided to go to college.* Now it's just a brute fact that there's a radical difference between those two. Nobody doubts that. Now what's the basis for that difference? Well, one possible basis for that difference is that there's a conceptual link between *persuade* and *decide*. And that conceptual link simply makes one of them an analytic sentence, because of the nature of the conceptual link. That's one possibility. The other possibility is what Quine said; it's a matter of deeply held belief, or something like that. O.K. That's two theories. Let's try them out. The guy who says there's a conceptual link has a task. His task is to work out the conceptual link and to show that it works for other cases. And show that the notion of 'cause' which is going to be in there shows up elsewhere, and has certain properties and applies to some other language, and so on and so forth. Well, that job people have done; a lot of it has been done, not everything. There's certainly a lot of evidence for it. The thing that everybody seems to have forgotten is that the other guy also has a task. He has to construct a theory of belief fixation, and that theory of belief fixation has to show that this difference is established. As soon as you raise the question, you see that that's hopeless. There's no glimmering of an idea as to how a theory of belief fixation could have made that difference. Now, it's very striking that what a whole philosophical tradition has done is to say the theory that's plausible, and has a lot of evidence for it, and people have worked out in detail, is wrong, and the theory that doesn't make any sense at all is right. It's only in the humanities that you can do this kind of thing. If anyone tried that in the sciences, they'd be laughed out of the room. It's really easy to be caught up in these moods of irrationality. I was for years. But if you stop to think about it, it's wholly irrational.

SAPORTA: I've never understood truth-conditional semantics. I've never understood the link between meaning and truth-conditions.

CHOMSKY: I think truth-conditional semantics is very interesting. It's certainly not the whole story. Take the Davidsonian type of truth-conditional semantics. Suppose we want to construct a theory of meaning for French. And we're constructing a theory in some language, so, we're constructing it in English, which we assume we understand, just as when we construct a theory of physics in English, assuming we understand it. That theory of meaning for French is going to have to prove certain theorems, and among those theorems are: "*Il pleut* is true if and only if it is raining." Now if a theory of meaning doesn't prove those theorems, it's not doing very much. He said that's all it has to do. We can argue about that, but at least it has to do that, and that's truth-conditional semantics. That's not so trivial to do.

SAPORTA: But truth-conditional semantics can never tell you the meaning of a question or a command.

CHOMSKY: I think truth-conditional semantics is a limited but significant . . . It's significant because even this is very hard to do. And when you do it, you get quite insightful results. You begin to ask the question, as Davidson did—that's the interesting part of his work—if I say "John ran quickly" and "John ran," there's some relation between them. How do I work out a structural theory so that it follows from "John ran quickly" that "John ran?"—and that's not so trivial. Even that's not so trivial. When you do it, you quickly. . . . The plausible answer to that is that in the case of *John ran*, there's a representation somewhere in the brain that there is an event of running, and John is its agent. And in the case of *John ran quickly*, there is an event of running and John is its agent and quickly is its manner. And if that's the representation, then you can go from *John ran quickly* to *John ran.* But that's not so trivial. Because there's a theory of events, which is not a trivial result. Maybe it's wrong, but it's certainly not trivial.

SAPORTA: I remember when I was a graduate student, the example that was sort of discussed was the impossibility of trying to understand the sequence *The king is dead. Long live the king.* You couldn't understand that.

CHOMSKY: Actually, that example doesn't seem too difficult, but other questions are too hard. Like most interesting questions. . . .

*　*　*

The phone rings, and Chomsky answers. I know he is scheduled for another interview, and it sounds like it might be the reporter for the *Seattle Times*, so I turn off the recorder and prepare to leave.

We obviously haven't finished, and Chomsky asks if I ever get to the East Coast. I tell him that I used to get to New York pretty regularly, but that I have less reason now, since a very close friend recently died.

Chomsky mentions a recent trip to England, and learning that people that he had expected to see had died. He mentions his feelings at the death of his father, the sense that some protective barrier had been removed. And I realize that I really have been asking the wrong questions. What I want to know, just as much as the political and professional, is the personal. The irony is that what Chomsky volunteers spontaneously would be virtually impossible to ask directly without appearing to be voyeuristic or morbid. How does one ask, "What were your feelings when your father died?"

Note

1. It is particularly fitting that this interview should appear in a collection of essays dedicated to Joseph Sommers, precisely one of the friends I had in mind above, and someone who gave considerable thought not only to the political context of literature, but also to the social and political functions of literary criticism.

25

Noam Chomsky: His Epistemology and His Ethics*

Introduction

The question of what the relationship is between Noam Chomsky's linguistics and his politics is one that has been discussed off and on since the sixties.[1] And, in fact, Chomsky has often been asked this question himself. So I have to make explicit a certain disclaimer. I am not claiming to know something about Chomsky that he does not know about himself. That is, this is not a case (as sometimes occurs) where the biographer knows something that the autobiographer does not know or where the analyst knows something about the patient that the patient does not know or where the critic knows something that the author doesn't (as opposed, for example, to Sinclair,[2] who claims, with regard to Chomsky's epistemology at least, to be able to discern a gap between what he "preaches" and what he "practices"). I merely wish to elaborate on his answer and perhaps put the question into a certain perspective that Chomsky himself, for whatever reason, wouldn't consider.

*To be published in *Noam Chomsky: Critical Assessment,* Carlos Otero, Ed. (London: Croom-Helm). Reprinted with permission.

Technical Expertise versus Common Sense

Let me say one thing first about Chomsky's answer when asked about the relationship of his linguistics to his politics because I think it is of some interest. He always maintains that whatever relationships there are are very tenuous and, at a very abstract level, very speculative. So, for example: "If there is a connection, it is on a rather abstract level. I don't have access to any unusual methods of analysis, and what special knowledge I have concerning language has no immediate bearing on social and political issues. Everything I have written on these topics could have been written by someone else. There is no very direct connection between my political activities, writing and others, and the work bearing on language structure, though in some measure they perhaps derive from certain common assumptions and attitudes with regard to basic aspects of human nature. Critical analysis in the ideological arena seems to me to be a fairly straightforward matter as compared to an approach that requires a degree of conceptual abstraction. For the analysis of ideology, which occupies me very much, a bit of open-mindedness, normal intelligence, and healthy skepticism will generally suffice."[3]

So, clearly, one reason for his reluctance to make definitive pronouncements in this area is his belief that these represent two fundamentally different kinds of inquiry. Whereas one might expect a certain amount of expertise in inquiry into the nature of language, there are, in fact, no experts in moral issues. That is, political and moral judgments are essentially questions of common sense. In short, Chomsky does not want to legitimize the view that one has to somehow be a professional in order to deal with questions of morality and politics.

Now, interestingly enough, there is an inverse correlation between the extent to which there is genuine expertise and the way in which certain disciplines focus on credentials. Chomsky often points out that when he is invited to speak to mathematicians, no one would think of challenging him because he does not have an advanced degree in mathematics. Whereas, when he spoke out against the American invasion of Vietnam, people were always questioning his right, on professional grounds. "You are a linguist; what do you know about Asia?" His answer, of course, was that one does not have to be versed in Vietnamese history and culture (which, ironically, he had become) to have strong views about napalm. So given his view that these are essentially different types of questions, the connections can only be quite weak.

Let me elaborate a little on the two types of questions because it seems to me that the distinction constitutes a first approximation to a fruitful way of characterizing the sciences and the humanities. Chomsky suggests that one kind of question is one that is theoretically interesting, that is, interesting because it bears crucially on interesting theories. The other kind of question is what he would call inherently or humanly interesting. A theoretically interesting question is one like, "Is there a point of light at the bottom of a mineshaft?" Presumably the only people who care are those scientists with a commitment to a certain physical theory. Conversely, the question, "How does one construct a just society?" is compelling, regardless of the absence of a relevant theory. So there are questions of theoretical interest about which one can reasonably talk about technical expertise, and then there are questions of human interest, which, for Chomsky, are essentially questions of common sense.

I think it is useful to compare Chomsky to Western scholars who have had the greatest intellectual impact in the twentieth century. Although there may be a danger here of some intellectual name dropping, my purpose is not to nominate Chomsky to some intellectual all-star team, but rather to ask, in a general way, "What is the connection between an important thinker's epistemology and that person's ethics?" Or, put differently, "What is the connection between people's attempts to interpret the world and their attempts to change the world?" Now, the names that typically emerge in such discussions are Einstein, Marx, sometimes Freud, sometimes Darwin. If one looks at the discussions of scientific revolutions, Einstein is cited as the paradigmatic example of modern times. If one looks at Kuhn's[4] discussion of candidates for scientific status outside the natural sciences, the examples he cites are Marx and Freud. Lieber[5] explicitly compares Chomsky to Einstein and Freud as examples of scientific "revolutionaries."

So if you ask about the relationship of Einstein's scholarship to his politics and generally about people in the natural sciences, the answer seems to be, trivially, that there is no connection; that is, one does not expect that any inquiry into relativity would have any obvious connection to the fact that Einstein was some kind of socialist. The two are merely independent.

This is not to say that scientists are absolved of all moral responsibility. Scientists' intellectual curiosity is not an absolute virtue, as Chomsky is wont to say. Scientists, like everyone else, have to assume responsibility for their actions, and they have no right to act as if the foreseeable consequences will not be harmful. This also does not mean that scientific discoveries may not have immediate social and political impact (the classical example being the Copernican revolution). But this is very different from saying that there is some kind of logical or intimate connection between a scientist's work as scientist and the scientist's work as social or political activist.

If you ask the question about Marx and again about anybody in the ideological disciplines, then the question of the relationship of their scholarly work and their political activism sort of falls by its own weight, since it is hard to distinguish epistemology from ethics. The distinction becomes blurred precisely because the epistemological questions are often politically motivated. Hence the question cannot be very clearly formulated.[6]

So it seems to me it is in the human sciences that the question can perhaps be most fruitfully and most illuminatingly asked. And it is significant, then, that the question is asked about Chomsky, and the answer is neither obvious nor trivial.

Others who are familiar with Chomsky both as linguist and as social critic have speculated about the connection but in ways that seem to trivialize the issue or, at best, focus on aspects of the question that are of marginal importance. Thus, Robinson[7] suggests that what he calls "the Chomsky problem" is not unlike comparing "Sartre writing *Being and Nothingness* and then his plays and novels." But the issue regarding Chomsky's scholarship, has, as far as I can see, nothing to do with another quite different debate about the relationship between politics and art, or philosophy and art.

Similarly, there are those who assume that Chomsky as linguist has a great deal to say about the language of politics. But when Chomsky points out, for example, the Orwellian nature of the change in name from the Department of War to the Department of Defense, this has nothing to do with theoretical linguistics. According to Chomsky, any critical citizen should have been alert to the mystification implied in such a change.

And, to cite one further example, the observation that there is a racial and social basis for the stigmatization of certain dialects is a truism that has no impact on linguistic theory, since it is obvious that a speech community is not linguistically homogeneous and politically, the observation is little more than an elaborate paraphrase of the axiom that ours is not an egalitarian society.

General Features of Chomsky's Intellectual Posture

Challenging the Assumptions of Any Debate

Before I say anything about the substance of Chomsky's scholarship, it is worth mentioning one or two general characteristics of what one might call intellectual strategy that are common to his linguistic and political writings, characteristics that are more than merely questions of style.

One characteristic is to examine the assumptions that govern any debate. In linguistics, this was dramatically demonstrated by the questioning of the assumption that the validity of theories was somehow determined by the explicitness with which those theories were arrived at, what were referred to as "discovery procedures." This constituted a devastating critique of structural linguistics and resulted in a very fundamental shift in focus away from the limited perspective of empiricism to a concern for biologically determined linguistic universals.

Similarly, in his political writings, Chomsky has always been concerned that the right questions be asked. Let me give one or two examples. There has been a discussion about the correlation, if there is one, between race and IQ. Chomsky is sometimes asked to comment on that discussion, and typically his response is, "Why are we asking that question?" That is, what interest is there in determining, one way or the other, whether there is a correlation between race and IQ? The question has, apparently, no scientific interest since the notions of race and IQ are biologically not very clear. Why don't we try to determine the correlation between eye color and IQ? That would make at least as much sense from a scientific point of view. And the question has no social consequences except on the most blatantly racist assumptions. In other words, only a racist society thinks that this is an interesting question.

Indeed, Chomsky is critical of the whole use of correlations as a pseudoscientific mode, arguing that statistical correlations are not generalizations at all; correlations are facts. In other words, there is a difference in logical status between a scientific generalization and a statistical correlation. So if you say that the angle of incidence is equal to the angle of reflection or whatever, that kind of principle, that kind of generalization can presumably be supported or violated by an observation. That is, you can find examples to support or violate that principle. But if you have a statistical correlation, whatever it is, men are taller than women, or something like that, that kind of "generalization" cannot be violated by an observation. If you find a very tall woman, it doesn't disprove or even violate the correlation. Statistical correlations are facts; they are not generalizations. And that observation alone constitutes an indictment of much of American social science.

To present another example where it was important for Chomsky to rephrase the question. During the Vietnamese war, there was considerable discussion about the legality of the war. Some people claimed that the United States should have gotten out of Vietnam because the war was not legal. Others, like Barry Goldwater, argued that the war was legal, that there were a lot of legal precedents for that kind of military action. And then there were some opponents to the war who said that it didn't matter, that we should not even be asking the question since we knew it was a bad war, and that it didn't matter whether it was legal or not. Chomsky's response was rather different. He said that, on the contrary, it was an interesting question, a question of some significance and importance to determine whether or not this war was legal, not because it would change our opinion of the war, but it might change our opinion of the law. In other words, it was not the war that was on trial; it was the law that was on trial, and therefore it was worth determining the war's legal status.

Chomsky was once asked to write an essay on the question, "Why students rebel?" Instead, he said that that did not seem to be the right question. The important question was, "Why is it that *only* students rebel?" Why, for example, weren't the faculty rebelling? The faculty of today were the students of yesterday. What is it about the transition from student to faculty member that somehow dilutes people's sense of indignation and outrage, so that given obviously immoral acts, they do not rebel?

One last example. There have been a number of articles recently about the connection between the university and business and how people are shifting their research to the private sector. About ten or fifteen years ago, Chomsky was interviewed by someone from *Business Today*. I don't know who the interviewer thought he was talking to. The first question he asked Chomsky was something like, "How can we improve communication between business and the university?" This was when students were picketing recruiters from companies like Dow

Chemical. Chomsky argued that one can't improve it; it's perfect. The university does exactly what's in the best interests of business. Improvement would be impossible.

Generally, he said that when questions cannot be satisfactorily answered, it is often because they have not been adequately formulated.

The Search for Principles

There is another feature of his writings that I think applies equally to his scientific and his political work, which I'll characterize merely as, "It's not enough to be right; you have to be right for the right reasons." In linguistics, and in science generally, there is an insistence on the distinction between description and explanation. In linguistics, it has been important to motivate the correct generalizations by explanatory principles. The distinction between descriptive and explanatory adequacy has been widely discussed, both in the linguistic literature and, more generally, in the philosophy of science. It is not always clear what the precise nature of the distinction is, whether it is qualitative or merely quantitative.

It is generally agreed, nevertheless, that *ad hoc* hypotheses, even if they are correct, are of relatively little interest. There is an interesting illustration of the consequences of such hypotheses presented as a scientific paradox.[8] Suppose someone proposes a hypothesis that there are no humans over one hundred feet tall. You start examining empirically, measuring people, and there are a lot of people around six feet, and a few people are seven feet, and they support the hypothesis. And now you find someone who is ninety-nine feet tall. Your inclination would be to waver a little in accepting the hypothesis. So we have a "paradox" in that a supporting instance in fact doesn't strengthen the hypothesis; it weakens it. But clearly, the "paradox" is a consequence of the completely *ad hoc* nature of the hypothesis; there is absolutely no motivation for positing one

194

hundred feet, as opposed to ninety-eight feet, or 102 feet. A principled basis would presumably have something to do with bone structure, and body mass and volume, and gravity, and I don't know what else, as a result of which one might come up with a hypothesis regarding maximum height. Thus, *ad hoc* hypotheses have this interesting characteristic that they can sometimes be weakened by supporting instances. In any case, Chomsky has insisted that in linguistics one must always search for explanatory principles.

Similarly, in his politics, it's not enough to be right. Here, the most dramatic example was his criticism of certain opponents of the Vietnamese war. For example, he referred to Mike Mansfield as "the terror of our times." Mansfield was a senator and one of the earliest doves who criticized the U.S. involvement in Vietnam on the grounds that the cost was too high, in terms of life, in terms of money, in terms of the divisiveness of our society, and urged withdrawal. For Chomsky, that was morally repugnant. The implication was that we had the moral right to be in Vietnam if only we could reduce the cost, if only we had spent half as many billions and killed only half as many Americans. (Note that the cost in Vietnamese lives was largely irrelevant for Mansfield.) To Chomsky, the purely pragmatic opposition to the war was unacceptable; it was the principled objection that would be significant.

Chomsky on Linguistic Scholarship

Theoretical Linguistics

Let me summarize here Chomsky's major claims about language: One, ordinary linguistic behavior is creative. Nonlinguists, and even some linguists have a little trouble juxtaposing the words *ordinary* and *creative*. For most people *creative* has a connotation of extraordinary. But Chomsky chose the word carefully. By *creative*, he means innovative and stimulus-free and, by implication, not subject to either mechanical laws, or even theoretical explanation. Linguistic behavior, being innovative and stimulus-free, results in the inevitable tension between rules or constraints on the one hand, and options or freedom on the other.

Second, there is a fundamental difference between linguistic knowledge and behavior, and it is the description of knowledge that is the proper object of inquiry.

Third, a description of linguistic knowledge requires positing an abstract, rich system of principles of considerable complexity.

Fourth, the development of such a rich, abstract system, when acquired uniformly—that is, by all members of the speech community in a relatively short time, on the basis of fragmentary evidence—suggests a rich biological component for language acquisition. Specifying what those biological constraints are constitutes the core of theoretical linguistics.

And finally, these principles are language specific. There is not a general principle of the growth of knowledge, but language contributes to what Chomsky would call the modularity of the mind, that language is one of a set of mental organs, another being vision, and perhaps others.

Linguistics as a Branch of Cognitive Psychology

As a matter of fact, it is commonplace to refer to linguistics as a branch of cognitive psychology. My impression is that such a characterization is a little misleading because it implies that there are other aspects of human knowledge, or cognitive domains where we have comparable theories. When one asks what those comparable areas are, the example that is usually cited first is vision.

Now, I have a little trouble with that one. Vision seems to me to be a characterization of a process, not a product. Consider, for example, the following. One aspect of our knowledge presumably includes what we know about physical space, that we live in a three-dimensional world, etc. That might very well constitute a cognitive domain. One source of evidence relevant for the growth of that piece of knowledge surely is the visual system. But someone blind from birth also shares much of that knowledge but, by definition, has used different kinds of evidence. The term *vision* seems to refer more appropriately to the source of evidence than to the cognitive domain itself.

The other example that is sometimes mentioned in this connection is a certain branch of economics about which I can't say anything. But if linguistics is a branch of cognitive psychology, it is surely the most advanced branch.

Philosophical Implications

Chomsky's inquiry into the nature of language bears on traditional epistemological questions regarding the nature of human knowledge and its growth and acquisition, his proposal being that language is one of a set of mental faculties. These faculties and mental organs might include knowledge of physical space, the world we perceive and live in, knowledge of mathematical concepts like numbers, or the relationship of part to whole, and, by extension, analogous to the universal theory of grammar, theories of aesthetics,[9] and crucially for this discussion, a mental organ regarding justice.

This leads to a not unfamiliar position, one that is controversial but certainly in a classical tradition: humans are somehow endowed with knowledge of what constitutes justice. This is in the tradition of Bertrand Russell, who claimed that we know what it is to be just, and furthermore, we know that we ought to be just. Or the question that Plato asked, "How can one recognize a virtuous act, if one doesn't already know what virtue is?"

Now, there are two related issues here. One is, What are the characteristics of this theory of justice? Second, What kind of evidence is going to be relevant in supporting a particular characterization?

A Theory of Justice

One type of evidence supporting any purported theory of justice is actually not unlike the linguistic evidence. We can construct a logically possible system of justice and then note that it doesn't occur; then we can speculate that one of the reasons it doesn't occur is that although it is logically possible, it is biologically impossible. Let me give an example: justice is not going to be the same as equality. That is, we can imagine situations in which equality would be unjust. A good example is the biblical story about Solomon and the two women who claimed to be the mother of the same child. Solomon's solution was to propose to cut the child in half. Equality, but presumably not justice. (The story would be better for me if both women were equally indignant. In the story, it's the biological mother who's the one that's outraged, which raises questions about maternal instinct, etc., but revise the story so that both people find the solution equally unacceptable.) Clearly, here is a logical solution that is biologically impossible.

Now substitute *food* instead of a child. The solution seems quite reasonable. There's another principle here, namely that human life and property are not to be equated. Substitute a pair of identical twins. There it's less obvious. Suppose you had a pair of identical twins, and Solomon proposed "Okay, you each take one." There we might disagree. But even the fact that a group of people might disagree, it seems to me, is not irrelevant. That is, there is a broad range of cases where presumably we do agree, a range of phenomena over which we understand that justice and equality are related but not synonymous and that life and property are not to be equated. But notice that if, in fact, there is a wide range of hypothetical cases about which we agree, that can only mean that we must have somehow internalized a similar set of principles; and there is no reason to believe that the similarity in these principles is merely a result of some common experience.

A similar argument is made by philosopher of law John Rawls, in a book interestingly enough titled, *A Theory of Justice*.[10] He asks us to imagine a society that convenes to write a constitution, that is, a set of principles for its governance. We are to imagine further that these people are typical, except that they all suffer from a unique form of amnesia; nobody knows who they are or anything about their own personal history. No one knows whether they are young or old, men or women, or anything of their own experience. Under that set of circumstances, Rawls asks, what kind of a constitution would they write? The second part of the book deals with the answer to that question. But the method is of some interest. It implies that people could somehow arrive at a consensus about a constitution, and that they would not, because of self-interest, bias the constitution for or against people on the basis of irrelevant characteristics like race or sex. In short, the process would be limited by their understanding of what would be in the best interest of the society as a whole, and furthermore, the proposal implies that this shared understanding of justice would not be the result of shared experience.

Positing a universal sense of justice raises a number of questions. One obvious question is, How does one deal with societies that clearly violate this common understanding? How does one deal, for example, with a society that legitimizes slavery? For Chomsky, such a society is what he would call "pathological." I think he means that literally; he's not using hyperbole there.

One of the objections to Rawls, which is of some interest to me, is the following. Rawls ignores what one might refer to as the "gambler's mentality." One could argue that there are some people who would risk, let's say, being slaves, if that meant that they might have the possibility of owning a slave. Even knowing that there is something morally objectionable, there are people

199

who are willing "to bet their lives." Presumably, for both Rawls and Chomsky, anyone who would risk some inalienable human right on a gamble would also be pathological. So both societies and individuals may provide striking anomalies.

But what such observations seem to address is the question that recurs in science regarding the relevance of counterexamples. Counterexamples may not be critical in overthrowing a theory. What is required is a better theory. The existence of counterexamples is of interest particularly when an alternative theory can account for them.

In any case, the constitution that Rawls proposes is essentially an elaboration of a theory that hopefully captures some of our pretheoretical intuitions about justice. The argument can be turned around. There might be some interest in examining theories that have been proposed that violate those intuitions. Consider, for example, two types of entitlement theory. One, which most of us object to, claims that brawn should somehow entitle a person to material wealth. There's something unacceptable about the notion that someone is entitled to beat you up and keep your money because they are stronger. On the other hand, if someone is smarter than you and cheats you out of your money, that does not seem quite so reprehensible. We find ways of rationalizing it. And, indeed, some advocates of a "meritocracy" explicitly argue *for* a correlation between "intelligence" and privilege, status, and material wealth.

So it might be of some interest to ask what the basis is of these entitlement theories. To what extent do they contradict our intuitions? How are they rationalized?

From Science to Politics

The Mind: Rationalism versus Empiricism

What I have been talking about so far has been narrowly

epistemological. That is, what Chomsky has been talking about is inquiry into the structure of the mind, and that is a question of science. The relevant objections, then, should be scientific in nature. That is, one can argue—and there's no doubt that Chomsky would agree—that most proposals about an innate sense of justice are too vague, they have to be made specific. The evidence is unclear, obviously. There are significant counterexamples; that's also clear. But ultimately, the way in which one replaces a theory is to provide a more compelling alternative. As far as I can tell, the only alternative to the rationalist proposal regarding biological structure seems to be some version of the "blank slate," so that essentially what is being argued is that the linguistic paradigm is irrelevant to other aspects of our knowledge. The narrow empiricist view, which has been so discredited by the linguistic evidence, seems to provide the only alternative when it comes to knowledge of ethics.[11]

In fact, it is my impression that in spite of all the lip service to rationalism and to the impact of Chomsky's work in linguistics, a large number of psychologists have failed to eliminate a substantial hard core of empiricism from their assumptions about human knowledge and its acquisition. So one hears the lay public talk about how "society *conditions* one to believe such-and-such" or how "attitudes are *reinforced* by society," etc., as if beliefs and attitudes developed as a result of conditioning and reinforcement. Obviously, one does not use the public's use of technical terms as a mirror of the discipline (people still say that "the sun rises in the east"); but I am not persuaded that, in this case, there is such a gap between the public and the discipline.

Political Consequences

It is at this point that one makes the transition from the epistemological questions to the political consequences. Positing a rich, innate concept of justice immediately raises questions

201

about the nature, need, desirability, and function of the law. What is likely to be the function of the law if, in fact, we have a rich, biologically determined system of principles that govern our views of justice? To the extent that there are biological constraints, then social constraints are at best gratuitous and at worst hypocritical. If it is a biological given that human life is unique and precious, then we do not need a law forbidding us from killing our neighbor. And, conversely, a law that legitimizes slavery is hypocritical to the extent that it blurs the distinction between life and property. We do not need laws either licensing birds to fly or prohibiting horses from flying.

Thus, Chomsky[12] shares with Rousseau the view that "civil society is hardly more than a conspiracy by the rich to guarantee their plunder." So it is only partly facetious to suggest that the relationship between justice and law is like that between universal and prescriptive grammar. The law more closely reflects questions of power than it does questions of justice.

What are the consequences of the distinction between social and biological constraints? Social constraints imply that human beings are perfectible, or malleable, as opposed to the position that claims that humans are self-perfecting; that's quite different. For example, when Chomsky was asked to account for the fact that so many people have quit smoking on the basis of behaviorist techniques of negative reinforcement, his reply is to ask how to account for the large number of people who understand that smoking is likely to cause cancer and as a consequence quit smoking. For Chomsky there is a fundamental distinction between coercion and persuasion; that distinction is critical, whereas for many behaviorists the distinction is fuzzy. Commenting on Rousseau, he says, "Thus, the essence of human nature is man's freedom and his consciousness of his freedom," (Chomsky, 1973, p. 391).

It is more or less clear that every political proposal is based, explicitly or implicitly, on some assumptions about human nature. The question I am raising is the corollary. Does every view of human nature have political implications?

Most linguists are familiar with Chomsky's review[13] of B. F.

Skinner's *Verbal Behavior*. About ten or fifteen years afterwards, Skinner wrote a book called *Beyond Freedom and Dignity*, and Chomsky wrote a review of that book as well (for an expanded version, see Chomsky, 1973, pp. 318–69). Predictably, Chomsky was not very sympathetic to Skinner's views of freedom and dignity. What Chomsky said is illuminating in focusing on the distinction between coercion and persuasion. He said that Skinner can answer the following question: "How do you get someone to say that the earth is flat?" That's easy. If you want someone to say the earth is flat, merely put a loaded gun to his head and most people will say what you want them to say. But Skinner cannot answer the question, "How do you get people to *believe* that the earth is flat?" Or, more interestingly, "How do you account for the individual, who, on principle, with the loaded gun at his head, refuses to say that the earth is flat?" That is, the person who says, "Go ahead, shoot! I'm not going to tell you where the secrets are; I'm not going to betray my friends." Those are the interesting questions, questions of belief and principle as opposed to behavior. To repeat, for a behaviorist, the distinction between persuasion and coercion and the distinction between belief and behavior are blurred, whereas for Chomsky, those distinctions are crucial.

There is an illuminating example of what happens when those distinctions do get blurred in government policies, or at least in the rhetoric of people in power. General Westmoreland, when he was commanding officer of the American forces in Vietnam, was told that his goal was to win the hearts and minds of the Vietnamese people; his response reportedly was, "Grab them by the balls; their hearts and minds will follow." That seems to be a classic denial of the distinction between beliefs and behavior or, at the very least, an expression of its irrelevance. Or, to put it differently, a view of human nature that fails to distinguish beliefs from behavior tacitly absolves people in power from the moral dimensions of their responsibility.

Free Speech: Linguistic Theory and Libertarian Socialism

Chomsky's political philosophy, what he refers to as "libertarian socialism," seems to follow, although indirectly, from his view of human nature. In fact, the linguistic model here is instructive, since it leads quite naturally to Chomsky's position on free speech. The imposition of constraints on "speech"—other than those that are self-imposed—is incompatible with the libertarian view. If, as Chomsky asserts, the ordinary use of language is stimulus-free, then it is equally true that it is response-free. People's behavior is not triggered mechanically by speech. There is no causal connection in either direction. Speech is not merely shouting, "Fire!" in the presence of fire; and conversely, humans are not sheep, driven inevitably to stampede by hearing the word *fire*, even in a crowded theater. You don't have to jump just because I say, "Jump!"

I assume that the issues illustrated by the classic example are in part reducible to the linguistic-ethical question of what kind of verbal behavior constitutes a "speech act." Thus, someone who says, "I will pay you to kill my enemy," cannot subsequently claim that such a verbal contract is protected by the First Amendment. Conversely, a baseball fan who shouts, "Kill the umpire!" presumably cannot be judged guilty of inciting someone to commit murder and similarly, I presume, for what is referred to as "incitement to riot." Chomsky's views on free expression are well-known. So, for example, Chomsky wrote:[14] "I have repeatedly and without exception taken the position that even authentic war criminals should not be denied the right to teach on political grounds."[15] Indeed, authoritarian constraints on what people may say constitutes, for the libertarian, a violation of one of the essential attributes of all human beings.

Political Philosophy

Chomsky's version of libertarian socialism is based on a rich view of human needs and aspirations, including the need for creative action, that is, action free of mechanical constraints.

How Chomsky's view of human nature leads to a particular vision of society is illustrated by the proposal that humans aspire to do productive work, as opposed to wage slavery, where they work primarily to avoid hunger. There's an anecdote that is told about Chomsky, which I think actually occurred, although whether it did or not is largely irrelevant. He was attending a conference with a colleague, and they were staying at a hotel. The colleague went for a walk and when he returned, Chomsky asked him what he had done. The colleague replied he had gone for a walk and had gotten his shoes shined. Chomsky said, "You mean you paid someone to shine your shoes?" And the two of them got into a discussion. The other person claimed that there was no particular virtue in refraining from having someone shine your shoes if the alternative is that they would have no work at all.

Finally, Chomsky asked, I don't know whether in indignation or frustration, "Would you pay someone to wipe your ass?" That is, presumably, there is work that is inherently demeaning and degrading, and in a just society, people would not be subject to wage slavery, that is, they would not have to choose between demeaning work and starvation. Now, we can argue about where to draw the line, whether shining shoes or cleaning someone who is capable of cleaning himself constitute demeaning work or not, but once again the principle is clear. It is simply not the case that anything people are prepared to pay for is therefore a legitimate form of work.

At the other end of the spectrum, committing murder for a living cannot be tolerated merely because there are mercenaries who are prepared to perform such acts. A principle delimiting the range of productive work is in fundamental contradiction, then, to the so-called marketplace mentality according to which moral constraints are presumably irrelevant, the pious pronouncements to the contrary notwithstanding. People in such a society get and are entitled to whatever they can pay for.

In the anarchist tradition, the just society would nourish the richest diversity, with a minimum of social constraints, using a metaphor that Chomsky borrows from Bertrand Russell: children are like flowers in a garden. What they need is earth and air and sun and the care which enables them to thrive. But one does not try to make a tulip into a rose.

The ultimate extension of this position is the proposal that groups would then form on the basis of voluntary association, and the principle of self-determination would govern decision making in the community and in the workplace, and indeed, virtually all aspects of daily life. Spelling out the details of that process constitutes the core of the anarchist program.

Conclusion

The strongest claim, which in fact no one is making, is that there is some logical connection between theories of knowledge on the one hand and visions of society on the other. Nevertheless, it seems to me, that with the developments in the last twenty-five years in the human sciences, and particularly with the beginnings of a coherent, comprehensive body of thought about mental faculties, it is now possible to pursue these questions more profitably than has been the case before.

Notes

1. In fact, about fifteen years ago, a former colleague, Stamatis Tsitsopoulos, and I gave a joint colloquium, entitled "Chomsky's Linguistics and Chomsky's Politics, or What do B. F. Skinner and Dean Rusk Have in Common?" That discussion was largely an indictment of behaviorism. It was easy to demonstrate that behaviorists were mistaken, and it was pretty easy to demonstrate that some behaviorists were also unethical; but it was not so easy to demonstrate that they were unethical because they were mistaken,

so that there were, in effect, two more or less independent indictments.

This is a revised version of a talk given December 1984 to the University of Washington Linguistics Colloquium, and it reflects the more informal style of that presentation. Earlier versions were presented at the University of Pittsburgh and UCLA.

2. Melinda Sinclair, "The Rationality of Chomsky's Linguistics," *Stellenbosch Papers in Linguistics*, No. 14 (Stellenbosch, South Africa: 1985).
3. Noam Chomsky, *Language and Responsibility* (N.Y.: Pantheon, 1979), p. 3.
4. Thomas S. Kuhn, "Logic of Discovery or Psychology of Research?," I. Lakatos and A. Musgrave, eds. *Criticism and the Growth of Knowledge* (N.Y.: Cambridge University Press, 1970).
5. Justin Lieber, *Noam Chomsky: A Philosophic Overview* (N.Y.: St. Martin's Press, 1975).
6. Consider contemporary usage of the word *feminist*, which is used to characterize both "a way of knowing" as well as "a way of acting," i.e., one finds references both to "feminist scholarship" and to the "feminist movement."
7. Paul Robinson, "The Chomsky Problem: Review of Chomsky (1979)," *The New York Times*, February 25, 1979, p. 3.
8. Martin Gardner, "Mathematical Games," *Scientific American* (March 1976): pps. 119–22.
9. That there might be a universal component to certain poetic phenomena is an ancient proposal, which has become rather unfashionable. Consider, for example, the use of the seasons of the year as a metaphor for the stages of human life. The fact that such a metaphor is so prevalent and so readily understood suggests that perception of the similarity is not 'learned' nor a function of some shared experience. For a discussion of music in a similar vein, see Fred Lerdahl and R. Jackendoff, *A Generative Theory of Music* (Cambridge: MIT Press, 1983).
10. John Rawls, *A Theory of Justice* (Cambridge: Harvard University Press, 1971).
11. In principle, of course, there is the Piagetian alternative view of rationalism, where what is biologically given is some "general intelligence." See Massimo Piatelli-Palmarini, *Language and Learning: The Debate between Jean Piaget and Noam Chomsky* (Cambridge: Harvard University Press, 1980).
12. Noam Chomsky, *For Reasons of State* (N.Y.: Random House, 1973).
13. Noam Chomsky, Review of B. F. Skinner's *Verbal Behavior* in *Language* 35 (1959): pp. 26–58.
14. Noam Chomsky, "Freedom of Expression? Absolutely," *Village Voice,* July 1–7, 1981, pp. 12–13.
15. I do not wish to exaggerate the applicability of the linguistic model, but if a sentence may be said to have both a meaning and a significance, then it is surely the latter that needs monitoring. If so, then one might reasonably ask whether or not a comparable distinction is crucial for our understanding—let alone legislating—nonverbal behavior. In fact, most legal systems either implicitly or explicitly do distinguish an act from a deed. For example, writing one's name is an act; signing a contract is a deed.

207

PART VI

LETTERS

26

University President's Essay Errs on Athletics and Priorities*

Editor,

William F. Gerberding's piece (*Seattle Times*, September 10, 1989) should be required reading for anyone genuinely interested in the status—some would say, the "demise"—of higher education.

The ideas that college athletes should be paid or that big-time athletics is somehow egalitarian are not new. But this isn't the self-serving rhetoric of a basketball coach like Digger Phelps (Notre Dame) or John Thompson (Georgetown); this is a university president.

Like most administrators, Gerberding's view of corruption is the "rotten apple" approach. The prevalence of booster payments, Mickey Mouse course schedules, and excessive use of steroids are not anomalies but the predictable consequences of a system that demands national prominence as the only measure of success. What we have here is not a few "rotten apples" but a "rotten barrel."

I agree with those who think that Michael Jordan is an athletic genius, who, as someone said, probably is playing in the NBA because he got cut from some team in a higher league. The pleasure and emotion generated by skilled athletes performing at their best needs no additional justification. But what Ger-

*Originally published in the University of Washington *Daily*, September 20, 1989. Reprinted with permission.

berding is defending is not the "healthy competition" between gifted athletes, but the perversion of that competition, like someone arguing for prostitution because for many, it constitutes the only available alternative to love.

Gerberding is right in pointing out the elitist nature of an earlier generation of academics. But what the contemporary university has done is replace that elitism with a veneer of egalitarianism, according to which, for example, the number of black athletes is presumed to be a measure of racial justice. Opportunism is a sorry substitute for decency and integrity.

Analogously, I suppose, the way to demonstrate our lack of bias toward women would be to recruit more of them into fields like nursing, librarianship, home economics, and elementary education. Indeed, we could provide scholarships and special admission requirements and then philosophize about why some of our most gifted nurses are economically and educationally disadvantaged.

Gerberding is quite charitable to the college drop-out, if he turns out to be an athlete. Even for those who do not graduate, "exposure to a university [is not] a waste of time or a squandering of our resources. . . . Society has an obligation to make these opportunities available." I agree completely. But Gerberding is talking to and about the wrong people. The scout for the Seattle Sonics couldn't care less whether that promising power forward has a college degree or not. In fact, they just signed someone who never attended college at all. Let Gerberding tell the recruiters from Boeing, though, that a degree is not necessarily a reliable barometer of an individual's education. They could have a good laugh over that one.

And, ultimately, that is the crux of the issue. Gerberding boasts about our greatest weakness: "We in higher education are the farm clubs for the NBA and the NFL. We are also farm clubs for commerce and industry . . . "* Twenty or thirty years ago, there was an expression of outrage when a corporate

*Excerpt reprinted with permission of the *Seattle Times*, September 10, 1989.

manager suggested that "what's good for General Motors is good for the country." But now we have tacit acceptance by the university that the corporate interest and the public interest are synonymous. If the president of the large university is right in characterizing the institution of higher education as essentially serving the needs of commerce and industry, then all the rhetoric about independent thought, and the life of the mind, and the pursuit of knowledge for its own sake is vacuous. Gerberding should be embarrassed to even talk about reading Plato.

Gerberding is quite sanguine about the possibility of "a national union of collegiate players who bargain collectively with universities regarding their financial support."* This is the same administrator who thought that a union for university faculty was uncalled for since we already benefitted from something far superior, a mysterious quality referred to as "collegiality."

One last point. Gerberding sees no evidence that the emphasis on athletics at a university results in "skewed priorities." I'll begin to believe him when he writes—and the *Times* prints— a half-page essay on, say, the status of the humanities.

*Excerpt reprinted with permission of the *Seattle Times.*

27

A Letter from a Former UW Professor*

Editor,

This hasn't been a really good year for me. In June, I was virtually forced to retire from the faculty of the UW because of a complaint alleging sexual harassment. Then, three months later, Boeing bought Longacres Race Track and announced that they would build a "campus-style" office complex there instead. In between, I tore a muscle in my back, trying to lift a box of books, after having been evicted from my office, and I was even denied a mail box—a petty, vindictive act by weak, mean-spirited men and women. That was just about the time that George Bush sent 100,000 American troops to the Persian Gulf. I think he was upholding the principle that Might doesn't make Right, but I may have gotten that wrong.

Except for my house, the university and the race track are the two places where I've spent most of the last 30 years. That my connection with both should terminate together makes a comparison inevitable.

The local sports columnists have devoted more space to the sale of Longacres than they had to the 125 days of racing that preceded it. (On getaway day, Ron Hansen came up from California and won five races; there was not a word about it in the *Seattle Times*.) Most of the coverage dealt with the "industry,"

*Originally published in the University of Washington *Daily*, October 22, 1990. Reprinted with permission.

the jobs lost, the revenue to the state, etc. There were articles on the Alhadeffs, Longacres' owners, who were portrayed as greedy, callous and unfeeling; that sounds more or less right. Joe Gottstein, who built the track, was referred to as a "humanitarian," which is the kind of rhetorical fluff one expects in obituaries, not in serious reporting. Let's get one thing straight: humanitarians do not build race tracks, and people who build race tracks are not humanitarians; what they are are legalized bookies, a term I use with affection, incidentally, not with contempt, which I reserve for academics.

There were references to the trainers and jockeys and owners, lip service paid to the mutuel clerks and waitresses and bartenders, but I couldn't find any reference at all to the effect that the closing of Longacres might have on the fans. Maybe someone should explain to the press what a "million-dollar-a-day handle" means and where it comes from. It's the fans who eat the lousy food and buy the overpriced drinks, and the programs and the T-shirts, and the key chains and the money clips. You get the idea.

What distinguishes a race track fan from say, the Husky football fan, is that the former is more gambler than sports fan. Everyone understands that without betting, there would be no "thoroughbred industry," and all the gushing about the "dreams" and "race track family" is useful mystification, more or less comparable to the rhetoric of university administrators who talk about nurturing the imagination and creativity of young people. Imaginative, creative young people are probably the single greatest threat to the contemporary university.

But precisely because the race track fans are mostly gamblers, they tend to be considerably more cynical, knowledgeable and sophisticated about their sport. So, they understand that one of the potential uses of legal drugs is to mask *illegal* drugs, that the use of illegal electrical devices is routine, and although never reported in the press, there is an occasional investigation by the stewards into a given horse's "sudden reversal of form," the prevailing euphemism for a fixed race.

And the same fan is amused, if not downright contemptuous, of attempts to "market" the track with buffalo races or horseshoe pitches. Whoever was responsible for introducing those ideas at Longacres took one too many courses at the UW business school.

What the fan wants, and what there is no substitute for, is the spectacle—dare I say "thrill"—of seeing talented, equally matched athletes competing at their best, like Sunday Silence and Easy Goer in last year's Preakness and having a ticket on one or the other.

So, a large number of the fans at the track are gamblers, touts, hustlers, and bookies, all with a touch of larceny in their hearts. They tend to drink a little too much. Sometimes they bet more than they can afford to lose, they yell and curse, and are blatant in their use of racist and sexist epithets. When they lose, which is usually, they have a long list of scapegoats to blame: the jockeys are crooks, the gate crew inept, and the stewards are incompetent.

In other words, when it comes to honesty, decency and integrity, the people at the track are one or two cuts *above* university faculty and administrators, who, by and large, are pedantic, careerist, humorless, self-serving and completely unprincipled.

I'll miss the classes. I'll miss the student who listened to my lengthy explanation of a technical linguistic concept, raised her hand and then said, "So what?" I'll miss the student who let me go on and on about how the human species was unique, and then pointed out to me that *every* species is unique; that's what it means to be a species. And I'll miss the minority student who came into my office and told me to forget about educational reform, that if I really wanted to help students like him, the best thing I could do was to get out of his way.

But I won't miss the faculty meetings at which a group of mediocre teachers pompously discuss whether or not to give tenure to another mediocre teacher. I won't miss administrators hypocritically rationalizing the exploitative use of underpaid teaching associates, while they simultaneously provide inflated salaries for "stars" who bring "national prestige" while they meet classes (I won't say "teach") for two or three hours a week. And I won't miss the transparently dishonest evaluations of a co-worker's publications, where no one will acknowledge that the scholarship is virtually unintelligible, so that the question of whether or not it has merit cannot even be addressed. And I won't miss the endless discussions about "curriculum" where the "student's interest" and the "benefit of the program" are routinely invoked as disguises for self-interest, privilege and comfort.

And, I'll probably manage to get along without the sanctimonious indignation of the knee-jerk feminists among my former co-workers, who gave new meaning to the word *collaborator*.

So, I'm sorry that Boeing didn't consult me before they made their latest expansion. I would have advised them to leave the race track alone and buy up the university. But then, they might have told me that they don't have to buy the UW since they already control it to a considerable extent anyway.

28

Comments on Sexual Irresponsibility
Reflect Political Climate*

Editor,

James Kilpatrick's column (*Seattle Times*, August 25, 1991) in praise of Morton Kondracke's condemnation of what they both consider today's sexual irresponsibility inadvertently reveals a great deal about the political climate of our times.

First, it confirms what thoughtful social critics have repeatedly pointed out, namely that the terms *liberal* and *conservative* have become virtually meaningless in trying to understand contemporary debates about social and political issues. On too many questions, the assumptions that the two sides share are much more significant than the trivial details over which they debate. Consider, for example, how the so-called liberal press, until recently, callously kept characterizing the slaughter of over 100,000 Iraqis as "a job well done." Celibacy for young people, what Kilpatrick piously refers to as "self-discipline and the postponement of gratification," is just one more illustration of the convergence between self-styled liberals and conservatives.

Second, Kondracke and Kilpatrick coyly refer to themselves as "prudes," but it is clear that we are expected to perceive them as "courageous" because they are prepared to "defend the old virtues," virtues that have been "abandoned" by sexually active

---

*Originally published in the *Seattle Times*, September 8, 1991. Reprinted with permission.

218

teenagers, who risk unwanted pregnancies, sexually transmitted disease, and their self-respect because they have converted "a sublime union of man and woman" (gays and lesbians, please note) into "a fun thing." Equally scandalous for Kilpatrick are the celebrities and entertainers who somehow seem to have gotten by without marriage, an institution, incidentally, that nineteenth-century libertarians called a "form of tyranny." Interestingly, the only ages given are for "Jack Nicholson, 54, and girlfriend Rebecca Broussard, 28." One is supposed to conclude, I imagine, that sexual partners who are not just two or three years apart in age are even more morally suspect.

The sexuality of the very young, and of the old, seems to be particularly disconcerting in our society. The anguishing about "black babies," "growing up on welfare," the "moral collapse" of our society, and the preoccupation with teenage pregnancy is largely a hypocritical disguise for society's discomfort over teenage sexuality. Public display of sexually based affection is a privilege reserved for heterosexuals of the same race, provided they are neither too young nor too old. It also helps if they are physically attractive. Ultimately, Kilpatrick and Kondracke's message is clear: "If you're not married, just don't do it." To characterize this position as puritanical is charitable, when what it advocates is mass sexual repression.

Finally, and in my view most significant, is Kilpatrick's extrapolation from sexuality to the rest of our society. "Everything," he informs us, "is sliding downhill. . . . Captains of industry cheat . . . bankers knowingly violate securities laws . . . politicians accept contributions that are just short of bribes." The logic may be questionable, but I think one should not completely dismiss the juxtaposition of the personal with the public. I have no doubt that George Bush, our former commander-in-chief, would find little in Kilpatrick's column to disagree with. We have come full circle from the sixties, and the liberal/conservative axis has provided us with a frightening ideology for the nineties: "Make war, not love."

29

Thomas, Hill, and Sexual Harassment*

Editor,
As someone accused of sexual harassment, my perception of the Thomas-Hill hearings understandably does not exactly coincide with that of most observers. Ultimately, what I saw were two blacks, trying to maintain their composure while being asked—forced, one might say—to spill their guts out, largely for the titillation of one hundred million, mostly white, voyeurs. Included were fourteen sanctimonious hypocrites, who had already revealed their interest in the "truth," when they accepted without serious challenge George Bush's claim that he had nominated a person on the basis of his qualifications alone, and when they refused to confront Clarence Thomas when he swore that he had never discussed *Roe v. Wade*.

Some journalists, like Michael Albert of *Z* magazine found Thomas's choice of the denial defense instructive and unexpected. Two years ago, I, too, would have been surprised. But sexual harassment, like many other offenses, is not one that is subject to mediation, negotiation, compromise, and resolution. Quite the reverse is the case. As the investigation proceeds, the positions harden, the rhetoric escalates, and as we have seen, the focus shifts to challenging one another's credibility, so that in the end, vindictiveness and vindication become surrogates for

*Originally published in the University of Washington *Daily*, January 21, 1992. Reprinted with permission.

justice. Thomas might very well have understood this and cynically opted for this alternative strategy: "Deny, deny, deny." After all, he had not previously impressed us with his candor or integrity. If he could not recall discussing legalized abortion, he was not likely to remember much about his interest in pornography, either.

But the difficulty, I would maintain, is not merely that people in high places lie to save themselves, but, more generally what Sheldon Wolin (quoted in Bill Moyers, *The World of Ideas*) has characterized as the "erosion of faith in democratic values. I've always drawn a distinction," he says, "between liberal values and democratic values. Liberal values are values that are basically suspicious of democracy. Liberal values stress the importance of constitutional guarantees, bills of rights, legal procedures, due process and so on, as protections against . . . popular movements. . . . The movement . . . toward liberal values . . . is ultimately a way of hollowing out the content of democracy." The adversarial nature of our legal and quasi-legal institutions makes lying unavoidable. Perjury constitutes no more of a moral dilemma than speeding. It is not only the nomination process that is flawed, as most commentators acknowledged. It is our whole system for the resolution of conflict that was exposed.

One of the Senators asked Thomas whether, if true, the allegations would, in his view, constitute sexual harassment. My recollection is that Thomas answered with one word, "Yes." So much for the "watershed debate" about sexual harassment. Hill and Thomas, and the Senate and the media all agree: what we want is for our men to behave like gentlemen. This is to be the cornerstone of the new sexual politics, a politics that frankly, does not seem to me to be either particularly emancipating nor egalitarian. Consider, in contrast, the response that Emma Goldman made to the feminists of her day: "The tragedy [of educated women] lies not in their having too many experiences, but in their having too few." That position cannot even be articulated in today's political climate, let alone debated. Goldman maintained that "the abuse of power" was a predictable consequence of the rigid hierarchies in our social and political institutions, and that therefore, the emphasis had to be on transforming or eliminating those institutions, including marriage, incidentally, which many considered a form of tyranny. Compare that perspective with the one that makes it a top priority for the boss to refrain from telling offensive stories in what quaintly used to be referred to as "mixed company." In the movie, *Duck Soup*, Groucho Marx, as the leader of Freedonia, sings about his political platform: "No one's allowed to smoke; or tell a dirty joke." A case of art anticipating life?

One aspect of the media coverage that I have not seen mentioned, is the proliferation of "experts," mostly academics, who have manufactured careers for themselves out of their professed "concern for women," a concern that, not surprisingly, is indistinguishable from their puritanical sexual politics. Among lawyers, counsellors, and academics, sexual harassment has become the growth industry of the nineties, replacing affirmative action as the focal point of the new sexual politics. Unfortunately, it is not always easy to distinguish political activists from profiteers. We have already heard some of them advocating a form of sexual apartheid in universities and the workplace.

Finally, not on the agenda, as far as I can tell, is the interaction of age and sexuality as they affect complaints of sexual harassment, an issue to which I admit a personal sensibility. The U. of W. *Daily* (May 29, 1990) quoted a student as referring to me as "someone old enough to be her grandfather," reported with no comment or discussion. Imagine, as a basis of comparison, a black faculty member, and a comparable comment about his skin color. The blatant racism would virtually discredit the complainant, since it would provide compelling evidence of a double standard. But, paradoxically, analogous bigotry towards old people is so prevalent that it is almost invisible. The "dirty old man" stereotype is as pervasive as it is pernicious. (Interestingly, my attempts to raise such questions during the investigation were dismissed as "intellectualizing," the irony of which will not be lost on critics of our institutions of higher learning.)

So, the issues involved in sexual harassment cases are not simply answering the question of "Did he or didn't he?" For starters, we might rediscover in speech, the distinction between what is offensive and what is coercive, a distinction that is apparently too subtle for people who enjoy being referred to as "militants." Sexual harassment is inextricably entwined with our ideas about sexuality, repression, censorship, power and process. That debate has yet to take place.

30

Family Values*

Editor,

Compassion, integrity, loyalty, and a social conscience. Admirable qualities that, as far as I can tell, are human values, that have nothing to do with the definition of family, or alternative life-styles.

But there are some family values:

1. No TV until you've done your homework.
2. No dessert unless you finish your vegetables.
3. Always take a sweater, just in case.
   And that focus of all family instruction,
4. Never, *never* leave the house without clean underwear, because you can never tell what will happen.

Furthermore, it should be clear that these noble principles can only be acquired in a household that has exactly two, heterosexual, legally married adults.

*Originally published in edited form in the *Seattle Times*, September 16, 1992. Reprinted with permission.